YOUR CHILD IS AN ARTIST

Pierre Drawing by Renoir.

YOUR CHILD

IS AN ARTIST

By ARTHUR ZAIDENBERG

GROSSET & DUNLAP *Publishers* NEW YORK

For
Wendy - Philip - Valerie
and Pierre

CONTENTS

COLOR ILLUSTRATIONS

FOREWORD

THE SOURCE OF ART is not visual reality but rather the dreams, hopes and aspirations which lie deep in every human. In childhood, limited experience must be coupled with lively imagination to meet the impact of the strange and wonderful adult world. This imagination, composed as it is of the unexpressed needs, hope and wonder, is by far the largest part of the child's conscious mind and all of his unconscious. It is from this rich source that a child evokes his drawings. Knowing nothing of "Art" conventions, as yet unacquainted with snobbery and chichi, bohemian pretenses or artistic ambition, the child's work is pure expression—a treasure vainly sought by most adult artists and rarely achieved by any but the greatest.

Somewhere along the route to adolescence most children seem to lose this ability for pure expression. It is the aim of this book to awaken parents to the value of the treasure possessed by their children and to teach those parents to help retain and cultivate that treasure. The title of this book conveys literally the opinion of this writer as well as that of an increasing number of art critics and amateurs, artists and teachers.

That many schools of psychology have dealt with the art of children at considerable length is of interest and significance and relevant to this book. But the obvious conclusion to be drawn from the phenomenal art production by children has only been lightly dealt with—the conclusion that the work spontaneously produced by children is indicative of a vein of artistic potential and "talent" inherent in us all and manifest in the "unspoiled" artistic statements by children.

This vein of creative potential in children is not a new discovery. It was Plato's theory that art should be the basis for education. Sensitive teachers have often observed with surprise and delight — mixed with troubling doubt as to the efficacy of ordinary teaching methods in evoking the best in their pupils—the rich and beautiful expression of imagination, emotion and wonder contained in drawings by those who are often indifferent students.

In so far as this writer has been able to observe from a remembrance of his own school days and from having watched with deep interest the educational progress of a large number of nephews, nieces and the children of friends, such art education as has been made available to him (in public schools) and to other children has been of a most perfunctory nature and even such infrequent contact with "art" as has been available was so lamentably misguided that it was not only ineffective but most injurious.

How to discover, encourage and guide the creative expression common to all children and well developed in many, is the purpose of this book. Should it serve to awaken even a few parents to the magnificent potential in their children, a potential for emotional release, cultural development, happy interest and possibly great contribution to the pleasure of mankind, this book will have been justified.   A. Z.

INTRODUCTION
By Dr. Herbert Kalmanoff

EVER SINCE the dawn of civilization, fond and doting parents have mused on the possibility that their newly-arrived offspring will become important, famous, great in some field. When these same offspring fail to measure up to these lofty aspirations, their parents regretfully assume that no unusual talent was present after all, that theirs were just average, run-of-the-mill kids.

But surely this is not so. There is a wealth of artistic talent lying untapped in the pudgy little hands and inquiring minds of our children— a talent that is never given a chance to express itself. You will see artists playing second base for neighborhood ball teams, paying their forty cents to see crime and wild-west movies, standing around on street corners after dark with the gang. Look hard enough and you will see an occasional Rembrandt, destined to live out his life never recognizing the amazing talent straining for release within him.

This world of ours can ill afford such a loss. Art, beauty, peace and happiness go hand in hand. In this book the author makes an eloquent plea to parents everywhere to give their children the opportunity to bring forth these attributes, to become artists, even great artists.

Psychoanalytic circles in general today consider art to be the result of a sublimation. Sublimation, simply stated, is a refusal by our conscious minds to recognize certain impulses as really existing in us, forcing the energy behind these impulses to be channeled off into other fields, which are generally acceptable. Thus it is believed that certain forces, motivations or tendencies struggling for expression deep down in the unconscious mind of the artist, which might have produced troublesome neurotic symptoms, are converted, instead, into valuable productions—works of art—by this process of sublimation.

We might almost say that Art is a compulsion. Having found his sphere of expression in Art, the artist is driven to bring some sort of harmony out of his inner restlessness. Painting is a reconciliation of his inner conflicts, which emerges as a pleasing composition, a concord, an agreement, and brings to the artist a sense of peace. An artist who unconsciously feels insecure, unwanted, afraid, often projects onto the canvas a feeling of security, of fearlessness. Art appreciation may well be determined to a large extent by the fact that if we scrutinize his painting, and have similar unconscious problems and conflicts as the artist, we will experience the very same feeling of relief and peace as he does, and therefore we will "see something" in the painting, we will "appreciate" it.

Unquestionably, artists as a class are not the only people striving for solutions of inner conflicts. We all are. And we all have been since earliest childhood. In this book Mr. Zaidenberg clearly sees the value of art for children, not only because it has vast possibilities for uncovering hidden talents which, like "full many a gem of purest ray serene, the dark unfathom'd caves of ocean bear," but because it contributes so largely to the growth of all the child's feelings and faculties, develops the creative instinct, the sense of freedom, self-confidence and self-respect; and also because of its medical value in both a prophylactic and therapeutic sense for our children, born into a neurotic world, and possibly destined themselves to become neurotic. He sees that as children begin to discover distinctive ways of expressing their hidden conflicts and repressions, their doubts and fears in art, undeclared hostilities and anxieties begin to emerge in both phantastic and objective form, and are resolved.

Children experience intense satisfaction from their art. It is a satisfaction derived from a feeling of achievement. It develops their personalities, leads to fuller lives. The quality of self-expression which art gives to them provides a mental satisfaction, for children love the feeling of having composed something on their own. They experience great pleasure from the play of phantasy in the subject matter of their productions, which brings them much-needed relief from the many anxieties inherent in their Oedipal relationships.

Do not dictate subjects to them. At first they may find it difficult to express themselves, but soon they will loosen up, develop a freedom of expression, and it then becomes clear that their subject matter has a very definite inner significance for them. They are now expressing the conflicts within their personalities, whose release on canvas may have a therapeutically beneficial effect.

From a prophylactic point of view, it is of great value to study the paintings of young children. It has been found that children of pre-school age express themselves with much greater spontaneity than those who already have been exposed to, and conditioned by, formal, inhibiting school requirements. Early and important symptoms of childhood maladjustment and neurosis can be recognized in the art of pre-school children much more readily than in that of older ones.

Adults are prone to misinterpret the art of children, chiefly because they see in it the art of adults, performed in an immature and inadequate manner. What they fail to realize is that the perceptions of children are organized in a manner different from their own. For children, the body is relatively unimportant, something on which to hang the really significant structures—the arms, legs, head. Instead of depicting what he actually sees, a child employs fancied characteristics and movement archetypes. The effects and emotions he evinces emerge in exaggerated contrasts in size and in clashes of color. Just as a psychotic frequently does, but for different reasons, the child often leaves out details which to him are unimportant, but which make his painting appear meaningless, lacking in composition and in artistic value to the adult. Incorrect proportions are usually used symbolically by the child, and enable him to experience certain emotions. He may place a tiny figure next to an enormous figure, thus expressing his helplessness in the Oedipal situation. When a child leaves out details, he is often expressing an emotion. Consider the naughty boy who drew his brother without legs and, when questioned, intimated that his brother would then be unable to escape parental punishment, whereas he, himself, would be able to run away. He is expressing on canvas his aggression and hostility to his brother.

There is a very close correlation between the child's art and his dreams.

As Freud has shown, the dream is used by us as a means of satisfying repressed desires, of experiencing guilt and punishment (so that these forbidden, repressed desires can then be allowed to gain satisfaction), and of overcoming great anxiety by its repetition in the dream, thus finally mastering it. The child, in his art, expresses his desires and his fears just as he does in his dreams. By means of the "Repetition-Compulsion" which Freud describes in his *Beyond The Pleasure Principle,* the child repeats, over and over again, his various fears, until he masters them by dint of constant repetition and ultimate familiarity. This is quite similar to the methods used in treating adult patients with traumatic (especially wartime) neuroses, where, by means of narco-synthesis under drugs or hypnosis, the patient abreacts the situation or event which led to his sickness, and eventually masters it.

When understood properly, therefore, we see that the child puts a well-nigh complete projection of his inner world by symbolic means on canvas, and that his painting is of tremendous aid in resolving the manifold conflicts of his inner world, and in developing his personality. Analysts working with them commonly find that children with difficult and painful personal problems, problems which they cannot communicate to their analysts in speech—troubled, morose, sulky, saturnine children—can actually work through their emotions and feelings, and develop into anxiety-free, happy, well-adjusted children through the medium of their art productions.

Finally, I believe that this book will be a most valuable contribution to the uncovering of vast amounts of artistic talent, which would otherwise have lain dormant. Surely a world that has progressed with such staggering—even frightening—rapidity in the uncovering of nature's scientific secrets, can be expected to produce more than *one* Da Vinci, *one* Michelangelo, *one* El Greco, *one* Van Dyke, to delight our senses. At the present time the potential counterparts of these masters are shooting toy tommy-guns, reading comic books and horror stories and going to "whodunit" movies. Mr. Zaidenberg offers, as an alternative, beauty and health.

TO THE CHILD

YOU ARE AN ARTIST. That does not mean that you are a "great" artist or even a "good" artist and it certainly does not mean that you have nothing to learn. It means that part of your natural ability, like the ability to think, walk and talk, is the ability to draw and paint pictures. Just as you had to learn to walk and talk, so you must learn to use the tools of an artist.

Let us first discuss what is an artist. Just to own pencils, crayons or paints and to use them does not make an artist. An artist must "say" something with those art materials. He must express an "idea" in drawing or painting.

This idea must tell something to the person who looks at it. That person must see through the artist's eyes a scene and, equally important, what the artist thought and felt when he saw that scene. In that way, the artist gives to the people who view his work the pleasure and benefit of the artist's eye and imagination.

An artist can paint a picture of a place he loved. A camera may take a snapshot of the same place in a far shorter time. But the camera can never tell you, as the artist can, how it *felt* about the place. It cannot give you the *emotion* of the artist. Emotion means love, pleasure, hate, or fear or any number of other feelings which are part of a person and are brought forth in his drawing. You see, the camera may act as another pair of eyes but the artist brings to people another pair of eyes *plus* heart, *plus* mind. The artist, so to speak, lets you in on his private thoughts about the place he drew and you become richer by his experience.

ACKNOWLEDGEMENTS

THE AUTHOR wishes to acknowledge the valuable advice and aid — indispensable in the making of this book — of the following persons: Dr. Herbert Kalmanoff, attending psychiatrist at the Essex County Mental Hygiene Clinic, and an associate of the Payne-Whitney Child Psychiatry Division of New York Hospital; Dr. Samuel Z. Orgel, fellow of the American Psychoanalytic Association, the American Psychiatric Association, the International Psychoanalytic Association, the American Medical Association and the New York Academy of Medicine, member of the New York Society for Clinical Psychiatry and consultant psychiatrist for the Jewish Child Care Association of New York; Miss Alma Paulsen and Miss Ruth Leider of the Child Guidance Bureau of the New York City Public Schools; Mr. Morris Finkel, Principal of P. S. 33, New York City; and the many children who contributed their fine drawings and paintings to this book.

The publishers also wish to acknowledge the cooperation of the Museum of Modern Art, *Life* Magazine, and Mr. Augustus Peck in granting permission to reproduce several of the full-color illustrations.

YOUR CHILD IS AN ARTIST

First Figure Drawing by a six-year-old

I. WHY ART?

THAT ART is, in a sense, actually the basis for most of our knowledge of the past, the great heritage of historic data and lore which we possess, is obvious. It is through the ancient ruins, architectural, monumental, sculptural and pictorial, that we know about great civilizations of the past. We know the daily habits, customs, modes of living and religious practices entirely through examples of art which have come down to us.

The ancient Mayans, Incas, Babylonians, Assyrians, Egyptians and very many other vanished nations are richly described to us by their artists. Anonymous historians and teachers were these artists, who little realized in making these sculptures, paintings and buildings that they were going to be virtually the only spokesmen for their time to people of countless future centuries. Undoubtedly, in these countries, there were also scholars, scientists and historians but relatively few of their works survived the vicissitudes of history and those which have hardly begin to compare with the works of their contemporary artists as visualizers of their times. Though less perishable, in spite of the diabolic ingenuity of man in creating forces of destruction, our own times will best be interpreted to future generations by our artists. It is they who mirror the essence rather than the superficial trappings of our civilization.

The foregoing is by way of justifying the existence of the artist, if such justification is necessary, from a purely utilitarian standpoint, that of

[23]

the historian. But you may be sure that, justified or not, artists will always be and will always serve as the mirrors and interpreters of their time.

As a means of release for emotion which, according to our psychiatrists' case books, often seek far less healthy expression, drawing has been recognized as a major therapeutic method. "Backward" children, schizoids and every variety of morbid personality are now being encouraged to draw and paint in order to aid in classifying their ailments, tracing the sources and giving channels for release of tensions.

These facts certainly imply to me that the "healthy" child can also use the release virtues inherent in art activity to help prevent and serve to express in readable terms the fears and evasions as well as the hopes and aspirations which are involved in the growing process.

The third "justification" for artistic activity is the aesthetic one.

To many (not most, fortunately) the painter is a parasite, one who contributes no useful work, a sort of immoral bohemian character who gaily starves while he makes pretty but useless brush strokes—when he is not wildly carousing in Parisian or Greenwich Village dives.

To millions of others he is one of the producers of that which is considered among the major reasons for living. Countless numbers of people regard the enjoyment of painting and the other arts as a justification for long years of work and struggle for existence. Many would readily part with all other earthly pleasures than those given by the arts—music, painting, literature and the others.

In these millions of "art lovers" the joy of appreciation could only be exceeded by participation, being able to create artistically. This pleasure is available to only relatively few. It is my contention that the potential manifested in childhood can be continued and developed if the importance of this potential is early recognized and carefully nurtured.

From early childhood on we are called upon to describe verbally our impressions of things. We constantly describe faces and figures of our friends and those of passing strangers—studied or fleeting impressions.

In childhood we learn to depict on paper that which we see, even before we are able to describe it in words and certainly before we are able to write descriptively. But unlike the process of spoken and written description, the power of graphic description is abandoned as we grow older and, so far as the

Painted in classes of the W.P.A. Federal Art Project, now on loan to the Museum of Modern Art, New York.

"*Circus Parade*" was painted by a twelve-year-old. Although there are too many stripes in the American flag, a famous art gallery was interested in buying the picture.

average man is concerned, completely lost. To my mind, aside from the creative aspects of art, the loss of this ability is the loss of a language. It is the loss of a means of communication by which one can reach everyone, a method of "speech" which knows no national boundaries or racial barriers common to the spoken or written word. How to foster and preserve unspoiled this native drawing "language" common to children is the problem with which this book is to deal. Of course, the approach is that of the highly personal viewpoint of this author. I do not claim the methods outlined here are the only ones possible. Each child presents a different problem and requires a different psychology and special handling.

But that the art produced by your child is highly significant both intrinsically and potentially is beyond dispute to my way of thinking. Its loss is a loss both to the child and to society, and its development is of value, surely, to the happiness and educational advancement of the individual child and possibly of enormous value as an artistic contribution to mankind.

Fascinating study of a school play area by a twelve-year-old French child.

2. WHAT IS ART?

A PAT DEFINITION of "Art" has never been formulated to the satisfaction of anyone but its formulator. To put into words the whole of the subtle psycho-aesthetic philosophy, mystic to some, material to others, emotional to all, is comparable to attempting to give a definition of the concept of God which will serve for all men and religions. I shall leave definition to other braver writers and restrict myself to a discussion of art activity—the production of expression in terms of the visual, on paper. Whether or not man is able to define art, all men are affected by some manifestation of it. The most primitive humans have always evolved through imagery an emotional expression. Drawn or carved symbols of their gods have served to expose their own fears and hopes.

Simple people everywhere are moved by pictorial delineation of their problems and interests. The symbols which move them are not always "good" art—often they are very bad—but each person is strongly affected whether by a poster or magazine cover or a Tintoretto Madonna.

Most people would disclaim an understanding of art. The common expression, often belligerently made, "I don't know anything about art but I know what I like" is really said defensively—a defense against the priesthood of artists and "art lovers" who for reasons of snobbery or by over-intellectualizing make art an esoteric religion for a choice sect.

[27]

But all peoples throughout history have been moved emotionally by art, either in their religious or secular life and usually, when presented with "good" art, they liked it and understood it. Granted the interest shared by everyone in some form of graphic expression, the taste and understanding of quality is what must be developed. Taste and quality are not absolute values. They are discoverable more by examples of their violation than by their pure presence. Just as in social behavior good manners are rather the absence of bad manners than a definable code of procedure, so in art one may say that good taste in emotional expression is that which does not violate the integrity or beauty or strength of that emotion. Quality would be that which is not defiled by the irrelevant, the vulgarity of overstatement or the weakness of understatement. In the process of creating art that expresses emotions in good taste and of high quality there must be brought into play all the rational and intuitive faculties of the artist.

To appreciate art the beholder must be prepared to employ the same faculties to the fullest. His own taste and understanding must be sifted free of banalities and prejudices in so far as he is able to do so. He must seek purity in understanding just as the artist must seek purity in statement.

That it is difficult to shed the vast accumulation of second-hand opinions and dull, ill-considered conclusions jealously held through vanity or fear of the unfamiliar is acknowledged. But that is exactly what one must do to enable one to recognize the valid, the pure and the beautiful. By the fortunate circumstance of having been relatively unexposed to the above mentioned accumulation of false opinions a child sees with the eye of innocence and thinks the same way. By innocence I do not mean vapid sweetness, for the psychoanalysts have shown us that children are encumbered with unconscious lusts, hates, fears and desires. The innocence lies rather in the fact that these basic emotions are innocent of second-hand philosophies, reservations, moral codes or compromise.

Great art is the rich record of emotional and intellectual experiences of exceptional people. It is obvious that somewhere in the early lives of these exceptional people they were presented with the opportunity and encouragement to begin to produce art or they never would have done so. Drawing ability is no more a part of the natural physical ability of man than is the ability to write script—and it must be learned in the same manner.

Not that "drawing lessons" are indispensible, but someone must give the equipment, encourage its use and above all justify the importance of art to the beginner. Who is to say how many "exceptional" people, never encouraged to begin, were lost as artists and directed into channels of mediocrity through lack of stimulus. How many potential "great artists" were thus sidetracked can not be estimated but it is certain that they are legion. As proof of the need of an atmosphere conducive to production of great art we have only to look at the Renaissance period to see how art grew and flourished and artists increased in enormous numbers in a small geographic area.

First figure drawing of a four-and-one-half year old New York schoolgirl.

3. TALENT IN THE
AVERAGE CHILD

THERE ARE, of course, many other factors which can be held responsible for the waste of original ability but chief among them is the belief, widely held, that only a few rare people are "born artists," that they have some mysterious "gift" with which destiny endows these biological sports and that some destiny "shapes their ends, roughhew them as they may." These talents received at birth are thought to be the invariable forerunners of inevitable "geniuses." This strange theory is responsible in a great part for the indifference with which the average child's work is regarded. Except for a few delightful experiments like those conducted by the Museum of Modern Art in New York where a free drawing and painting studio is made available to children in which they may scribble and daub as they please under the eyes of a highly appreciative audience, and the art-play of kindergarten play classes and a few progressive schools, the inventive child paints for unresponsive, disinterested eyes. Aside from these rare exceptions, the indifference to all but the obviously flashy talents has resulted in a loss of an incalculable wealth of art to the world and undoubtedly among the innumerable artists who never produced were many of stature potentially comparable to Titian, Michael Angelo, Cezanne and Picasso.

It must be admitted here that this theory can only be proved by an enormous increase in intelligent fostering of the art expression of millions of children and by our watching the results over a period of time. As an experi-

[31]

ment in prospecting for such real wealth, the undertaking should be well worth while. But until governments are willing to undertake such elaborate programs we must depend on the interest of those close to the individual child.

It would seem, therefore, that it is with the parents that one must begin in training the child to learn to use and continue to use this creative expression. The school teacher reaches the child later and, knowing little of his background and special psychological needs, must inevitably be in a less advantageous position to aid him. Since it is up to the parent to begin this task it would follow that the parent must be trained to do it properly.

Before the age of five all children begin the scribbling process when given a crayon or pencil and these scribbles are of real interest to the child psychologist. He uses them as highly significant data in judging the I. Q. of the child. The drawings of even two-year-olds indicate the amount of coordination and imagination possessed by the child. The strength and continuity of each line is instructive to the psychologist and this in itself should indicate to the parent the importance of graphic expression. But it is usually at about the age of five that coordination of the hand, eye and mind enables the child to use conscious expression in his drawing and it is at that time that parents should begin their observance of this phenomena.

What to do about it? How to analyze the virtues or faults? How to help and, above all, how not to hinder and spoil your child's instinctive talents are some of the problems to be taken up in the following pages.

Until relatively recently the suggestion that a greater part of the school day curriculum be devoted to the appreciation and practice of the arts, painting, music and the dance and other aesthetic studies was considered an encroachment on the really important studies—mathematics, science, history and languages.

Important as the last named studies are to our daily life and work, and certainly indispensable in any educational program, there arises the question of what is their relative importance in comparison with training in the arts to produce an integrated individual equipped to "live" in the richest sense of the word.

It only requires an examination of the lives of our friends and acquaintances to find comparison material for a study of the worth of a wholly "utilitarian" education, i.e. one devoted to the study of such subjects as will fit one into a successful career in business or science exclusively, as against an education which not only produces the competent, useful man but brings forth the man himself, in his richest potential, creative and appreciative of creation, able to express his emotions and understand the emotional expression of others.

The man educated from early childhood in a full appreciation, and more important still, the production of art work, will be the richer individual with healthier outlets for his emotions. To me the answer is indisputable. The man trained in appreciation of the arts and involved in their practice is immeasurably richer in terms of real values if not in material ones—though it does not follow that he will inevitably be materially poor if he understands art or creates artistically.

We will not deal here with art as a profession or a means of livelihood, although there are many thousands of artists who live by their work and find it not only lucrative but highly respected as a profession. We are rather concerned with this rather intangible term "artist" used in the sense of one who expresses himself in artistic language.

As a medium of emotional expression the graphic arts are accepted beyond the need of proof. We are all, without exception, affected by graphic delineation in our journals and schools and churches, by ways different from those of the spoken and written word—and often far more effectively.

Unfortunately, this means of emotional expression has been relegated to the "professional" artist, who no matter how proficient or even "great" can only speak for himself and his own emotions. Most people achieve their pleasure from recognition of those emotions but are unable to give graphic "tongue" to their own.

It is my contention that this language, native to every child, lost in the inadequate educational process, can be reacquired. That it certainly must be encouraged and continued in childhood should be obvious. Apparently it is not obvious, however, for—except for the "talented" child occasionally allowed to study "art"—the vast majority of parents and teachers allow this rich medium of self expression to slip into a limbo of disuse or at best relegate it to the few perfunctory "drawing classes" of the elementary school and the formalized dullness of the one hour per week class of the higher schools.

Lost or ruined is the free simple expression in line native to every child.

WRITING

Here is an example of the use of the same dexterity with which one writes script, applied to drawing and design.

4. WRITING

THE INVENTION OF WRITING, the use of drawn symbols to represent the spoken word, is probably the most important invention of all time. It is a comparatively recent invention when regarded in relation to man's history on earth. But with the invention of writing, man's real development began. Without a means of recording experiences, man's inability to pass on information to his fellow man except by word of mouth, directly delivered, hampered the growth of civilization.

Communication by signs, called hieroglyphics, was the form of drawn communication first conceived. Little pictures, at first literally signifying the story to be told, made up the prehistoric man's writing method. These picture stories have been found in large quantities on cave walls in various parts of the world and they depict the hunting, fighting, living experiences of peoples who left no other record of their existence except some stone arrow heads and crude utensils.

The drawn language, however, was often of such high quality that these people undoubtedly can be called artists. So fine are some of these drawings that they have been of considerable influence in some branches of modern art. The people who executed them, however, surely knew nothing of the refined cultural activity we call "art." To them it was another means of talking and when one considers the large number of such drawing talks that

[35]

have survived, implying a vastly greater number that time has obliterated, the practice must have been a common one, not restricted to specialists.

As man's civilization developed, the telling of a direct story in literal pictures, in reality by sign language, became replaced by the use of symbols. These drawn symbols meant more than the object which they represented, for shadings of meanings had entered into language and talk required more than the pictures of things. People had to learn symbols collectively used and the drawn writing method lost its direct illustration quality.

Script evolved as a quicker symbol system and the common practice of drawing lost its direct, daily usefulness and became relegated to the less immediate uses of decoration and finally, as in our time, a specialist's "cultural" activity. But let us look at this script that evolved from the original drawn symbol. Curiously enough, most people take for granted this extraordinary ability to write a flowing script.

Very rarely do we stop to analyze the fact that virtually every literate person has developed wonderful manual dexterity and a facility at making beautiful line drawings.

Years ago writing script was taught more as a fine art than as a means of visual education. Variations in the weight of line, shadings and flourishes were taught with a view to making script a graceful visual art. The angle of the script, the design of each letter and the grace of the T crossings were as important as the function of script to express meaning.

This over-stressing of the importance of beautiful script as the equipment of an educated person would be absurd in modern times where the greatest part of correspondence is performed on a typewriter and mere superficial grace of penmanship is less important than the thing to be said. But it is significant that most people were able to learn to perform these highly perfected Spencerian and Palmer methods of writing although they called for a high degree of manual coordination and skill.

This motor skill is an important part of drawing and is no more difficult to acquire than is a skill at penmanship.

This painting is the work of a well balanced 6-year-old child. The harmonious background, the architectural solidity of the composition, and the vivacious colors indicate an inner security and a healthy sense of freedom for self-expression.

5. AGE AS A FACTOR IN CHILD ART

A CHILD of three or four has, for want of experience with conventional symbols, special symbols of his own with which to express his ideas and contrived for himself alone. The vaguest scratches he makes have real meaning to him although they may convey nothing to you. A scrawled line may be a man to him and while an attempt to correct his concept into more conventional style might succeed, it might well be at the risk of losing the impetus which prompted him to draw the man the way he "saw" him.

In this respect a child's work sharply differs from the work of an adult primitive for the latter tries to be realistic but fails through lack of knowledge of methods. He would *like* to draw correctly. To him drawing is a method of communication which he consciously uses, though the results are always deeply involved with unconscious drives.

One must not laugh at the weird viewpoint of the young child's first efforts nor must correction be superimposed on the first drawing.

The danger that the child will lose respect for his work through damage to his ego is a very real one. His ego is an important adjunct to his progress. At that early stage of his development the urge to "show off" is comparable to the pride of an explorer who comes upon hitherto undiscovered territory. Therefore, while unqualified praise is not desirable, you must show respect for his efforts and spur their continuance.

Encourage him to save his drawings and, as they accumulate, his progress will show in direct relation to his mental development. Encouraging him to keep his work or accepting it gravely as a gift when he offers it is of invaluable aid in justifying his continuing with his drawing.

At the age of five virtually every child can draw as well as Rembrandt could at the same age. At ten probably about fifty per cent can draw as well as the master was able to at the age of ten. At fifteen the percentage drops sharply to about 10 per cent, and thereafter only other "geniuses" could keep up with him. Some special set of circumstances and conditions prevailed in his case which brought into life an ability which certainly was not always there.

Exactly what these circumstances and conditions were or should be to produce a "genius" can hardly be put into simple categories of procedure. The innumerable contributing factors are far too subtle and obscure.

We can, however, easily define the obstacles which are obviously detrimental to the pursuit of art as a life work. And if these obstacles are removed and the development of the urge to create is encouraged we at least have progressed the first few steps toward the making of a good artist and possibly a "genius."

In studying the drawings done by various age groups in England, France and the United States, it is interesting to note that at the age of about five most children do work which is freshly expressive of their observance of things about them. They are completely uninhibited and uninfluenced and these statements, though crude, are intelligent far beyond their intelligence as revealed through speech and action.

As the groups grow older the number of spontaneous drawings becomes fewer and they show more outside influence. Though less crude, the drawings become tainted with the conventions of "grown-up art" which they see in their cartoon books, comic strips and animated films. Their self-consciousness also develops and they are increasingly aware, year by year, of what people will think of their drawings. Spontaneous expression becomes calculated exhibitionism. Drawing, instead of being the direct language of otherwise inexpressible impulses, becomes a means of "showing off."

In most cases this deterioration of pure expression continues progressively until the original rich source of graphic speech is engulfed by extraneous, copied mannerisms. This process of gradual ruin is usually aided by the lack of understanding and encouragement given to the early efforts due to the failure of parents and teachers to appreciate the untutored simplicity of these efforts. Most adults, having themselves gone through this ruinous metamorphosis from the beautiful to the dull, ridicule the crude distortions of the early drawings and praise the progressive steps to "realism" laboriously copied from lifeless periodical and advertising "art."

The Austrian, Dr. Cizek, was among the first to introduce the theory that the teaching of art to children was a process of encouragement of the use of an instinctive language to be intuitively learned. The effect of this idea on certain schools of child education resulted in some amazing production of child art.

Painted by a ten-year-old boy this still life is as romantically sensitive and emotional as the mystic paintings of Odilon Redon. Vibrant lines and dramatic lighting, undisturbed by extraneous detail, make this worthy of a mature artist.

6. MODERN ART AND CHILD ART

THOSE WHO DERIDE "Modern Painting" often hurl what they consider to be the ultimate in insults—that it is like the work of children or aboriginal primitives.

Picasso, Matisse, Braque, Miro, Chagall, Klee and countless others are accused of regression to the infantile and the uncivilized. The accusation is not without some justification and these men, I venture to say, do not consider themselves insulted. According to their writings and statements, they struggled long and studied deeply to arrive at that state of purity which would allow them to see with the clear, original vision of children and to paint these visions.

At this point I hasten to state that the fine work created by these artists resembles that of children only in the simple directness of their vision, shorn of superficial manual dexterities and academic conventions. They did not at that point cease to be sentient, intelligent adults and their mature sophistication and rich emotion is apparent in their work to all those who, without previous prejudice, bring mature judgment to the examination of these works. If these artists need any additional justification beyond that which their paintings amply give them, it is only to refute the nonsensical implication that they work as they do because of the lack of technical efficiency to enable them to achieve conventional realism.

[41]

The early work of Picasso during his romantic "blue" and "pink" periods contains sufficient evidence of pure technical dexterity to embarrass even his most conventional critic. Matisse likewise was an academic art student of extraordinary technical attainments.

All of the other artists mentioned have at one time or another displayed work indicative of ability which, should they so desire would enable them to emulate and surpass their academic contemporaries in their own media. That they do not follow in the conventional pattern of these fossils of art is at once the despair of the dull and mankind's good fortune.

Primitive people, untouched by civilization's compelling influences, also partake of the vision and wonder of children—and their arts have been a rich source of inspiration to modern painters. Darker emotions, starker passions move the primitive native than motivate the child but the same naive wonder and simplicity is characteristic.

A study of the work of aborigines, whether African or American Indian, will be very instructive to one interested in understanding some of our most modern painters. These men are not children and when their work most resembles that of a child it is well to seek the important differences, differences which make the adult "child-like art" greatly superior.

As we have mentioned before, artists express their emotional and physical experiences and it is unreasonable to suppose that the richness and depth of emotional experience of an intelligent, sentient adult can be matched instinctively by a child. Conversely, however, it is plain that the art of children contains some of the important ingredients which the adult artist puts into his work plus a degree of sensitivity, courage and wisdom which cannot reasonably be expected in the work of a child.

THE FOLLOWING PAGES SHOW DRAWINGS BY CHILDREN *which demonstrate remarkable similarity in feeling to the work of fine modern artists, though they, of course, lack the sophistication and discrimination of the mature artists. ....*

A markedly modern approach is shown in this imaginative portrait by a twelve-year-old girl.

PICASSO

Always inventive but often traceably derivative in source, Picasso went to the primitives of Africa for inspiration for this phase of his work.

He foregoes, in this head, the use of the clichés of academic feature drawing, which were the stock in trade of the academic artists of Paris, in order to intensify the whole.

This work of a ten-year-old American boy might well have been the work of an African aborigine or an adult modern painter.

[44]

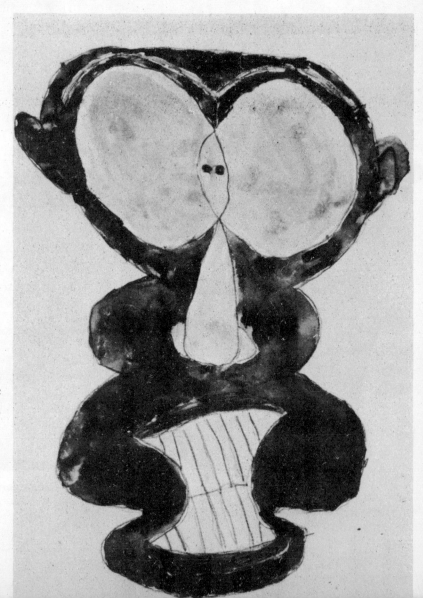

BONNARD

This delightful Bonnard has the very essence of the child's concept combined with the intelligence of an adult artist and is strikingly similar to the spirit of the work of the eleven-year-old girl shown above.

[45]

PICASSO

The work of this young New York child shows a remarkable kinship of feeling with the Picasso, to the left, which the child most certainly has never seen.

MATISSE

Matisse brings mature taste to simple and "right" design. Children often, through sheer unspoiled vision, capture something of the pure beauty of Matisse's work.

[47]

DUFY

This sophisticated Dufy utilizes knowingly the directness which is so characteristic of the approaches to a similar theme done by children in the plates which follow it.

[48]

KLEE

A Paul Klee line drawing and a drawing by a fourteen-year old boy.

[49]

BATTLE

A drawing by a fourteen-year-old boy after having looked at Mr. Hayter's drawing for several minutes.

COMBAT

An etching by Stanley William Hayter

[50]

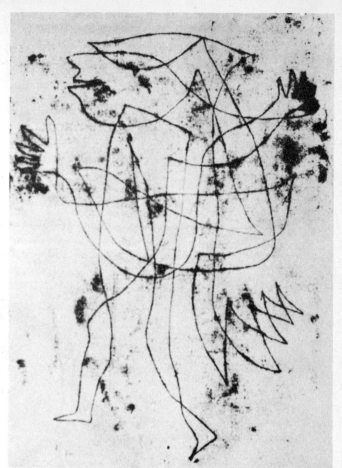

KLEE

The art of Paul Klee is the work of a mature artist which has, when examined superficially, characteristics which resemble the work of a child.

Always amusing, often enchanting, the tendency to simplify to the extreme and the scanty texture of his works often lead to the mistaken conclusion that they are the products of a childlike mind. Quite the contrary. They indicate a deep deliberation and a considered and strongly felt emotion.

[51]

KLEE

Here is another example of the work of a fine modern artist, Paul Klee, whose simplicity of line has often been likened to the work of children—together with three examples of child art, similar in approach but lacking in the high degree of sophistication which marks Klee's art.

Collection of the Museum of Modern Art

These two examples of child art are notable for their simplicity of line and directness of imagery.

BRAQUE

    Two examples of tasteful black-and-white spotting, one by the noted modernist, Braque; the other by a comparatively untutored twelve-year-old.

[54]

PICASSO

These wonderful cows are placed on a landscape that
has a highly individual set of clouds and a weird and witty
tree. Reproduced at the left is a Picasso tree which has the
same invented character.

[55]

UTRILLO

Utrillo's street scenes reached the height of sophisticated refinement and yet retained an almost childlike simplicity. Not the result of naiveté but rather of taste and sharp discrimination, these paintings drew the scorn of his early contemporaries and of the academic critics for their "infantile simplicity." Note the similar economy and sensitivity in the work of a child artist shown above.

[56]

This remarkable impressionistic drawing of Mont St. Michel by a serious-minded French schoolboy, curiously enough, only received a mark of 6 out of a possible 10 from his teacher.

A fascinating experiment in figure and animal drawing by an eight-year-old girl.

7. HOW TO ENCOURAGE YOUR CHILD

PARENTS should present their children with pencils, colored crayons and colored chalks at the earliest possible age, even at the risk of damage to the wall paper. Early beginnings in drawing are healthy both in developing mental and physical coordination and in forming habits of drawing and familiarity with the tools. When the child is most impressionable and has developed few other interests he will readily take to this medium of speech even while his tongue is unable to form words.

One cannot "teach" drawing to a child, for the stages of study to which an adult can apply himself are manifestly unsuited to children. One can only prepare him *to teach himself* by supplying him with the tools, stimulating his interest, acquainting him with the importance of art and leading him on the natural graduated stages of his growth process into more and subtler artistic creation.

There are, however, methods of improving his dexterity, manual and mental, correcting his most obvious misuse of materials and suggesting paths to follow, i.e., those along which he has shown the most aptitude in his earliest efforts.

Added to these positive approaches to aiding him on his creative way are the "dont's" which a parent must impose upon himself. These take the form of self cultivation in order not to misguide the potentials of the child. The "dont's" must prevent you from surrounding him with bad pictures in his home, suggesting second-rate pictures to copy and praising work of bad taste because they are "popular" and done by "successful" men.

[59]

8. ART MATERIALS

IT SHOULD BE BORN IN MIND that a child does not have the respect for "art" to the same degree that the adult has acquired it by long conditioning through talks with pompous "art lovers," magazine articles and trips through majestic museums. The respect for good art materials that comes with the respectful adult approach is sadly lacking in children. Crayons and paints are regarded as toys rather than serious tools to a serious end. I am, of course, referring to the child of four and five. At about the age of six he becomes more conscious of "personal property" and that is the time to begin inculcating a respect for his tools.

Since a child is likely to be very prolific and also wasteful it is certainly unnecessary to give him the best art materials available. They are expensive and more important still, they should not be misused and wasted. Nothing is more painful to the serious artist, usually poor in worldly goods, than to see the careless dilettante carelessly wasting materials which he, the artist, loves and uses with an economy only forgotten when the needs of the picture dictate. However, give the child adequate materials for free expression, for he has many things to contend with and one should not add to his problems by supplying unsuitable and incomplete art materials.

Above all, give him plenty of materials, lots of paper and many pots of paint and a wide variety of pencils and crayons for he will be induced to experimental and uninhibited productivity by a relatively unlimited supply.

Put at his disposal paints and drawing materials. Large brushes and large sheets of paper will encourage him toward freedom of expression. Try to find a spot in your home where he can have a work table or easel, a small chest for his paints—and unhampered freedom to splash paint.

For painting, I would suggest the jars of prepared "poster colors" which are bright, relatively inexpensive, and can be obtained in a wide range of colors. He will need a preserve jar for water and one to hold big brushes. A drawing board on which to tack the large sheets of paper can easily be made from an old table top or bought cheaply.

Paper for painting in poster colors may be either charcoal paper or stock drawing paper from the art materials dealer. Shelving paper which is sold in rolls makes a very good inexpensive sketching material.

The color grease crayons sold in all stationery stores are fine for drawing, better than colored pencils which tend to produce too fine and finicky lines. A number of soft lead pencils and a gum eraser are also needed.

Expensive materials are a waste and even a deterrent to child art. Quantities of vivid colors of the dime store variety are often more conducive to bold work than are the dainty, costly "sets" sold in many art shops.

Get your child plenty of basic colors — they are sold in jars — broad brushes and large sheets of cheap white or colored papers. Pencils should be many, soft, and expendable.

Crayons are cheap and so are colored chalks and they are preferable to imported pastels for free expression.

Though it means a risk of his clothes and your furniture, inks in rich black are a fine impetus to strong work. Pen or brush may be used with ink. Inks also may be obtained in color but they are usually pale compared to pigments.

Avoid oil paints for the very young. They represent too much of a problem. However, for children over ten oil paints often produce startlingly good effects. In France I have seen whole classes of ten- to twelve-year-olds painting with oils and doing fine things.

Help him choose his favorite medium by trial and error. The cost is relatively small and the adventure is exciting and stimulating.

BASIC MATERIALS

PENCILS: lead pencils #2 to #5 drawing; assorted color pencils.

POSTER COLORS: a set of jars of opaque water colors.

WATER COLOR SET: an inexpensive box of assorted cakes of color soluble in water.

BRUSHES: about five camel hair brushes #2 to #6.

CRAYONS: Five-and-ten cent store grease crayons of assorted colors.

CHALKS: large flat sticks of American pastels—inexpensive and colorful.

PAPER: many large sheets of drawing paper and water color paper.

DRAWING BOARD: about 24″ x 36″.

STUDENT'S EASEL

WATER JARS, MUFFIN PAN FOR MIXING, PAINT RAGS.

This forbidding fantasy was painted by a "tough guy" — a boy who had become a bully in self-defense against his environment. His rage and hate find release in his use of fierce colors, and in the exotic figure which he places against a background of striking dragons.

9. SKETCH HABITS

VERY FEW ADULTS "take up" a musical instrument, most musicians having learned the use of their instruments in childhood when new learning and development of dexterity come easiest. Yet most artists will tell you that they decided to become painters somewhere late in their teens and began to learn the rudiments of the "techniques" at a time when they found the drudgery of study held them back when they had much to say and were raring to go.

Habits are also most readily formed in childhood and once acquired are never a chore but part of a behavior pattern. The sketching habit is one that, learned in childhood, will contribute to the gradual development of technical dexterity, and the amassing of innumerable drawing experiences. If cared for, the childhood sketches represent a diary and a source of research of immeasurable value. The presentation of the first sketch book, preferably a bound one, should be made a significant occasion and each subsequent book should represent a step in the child's progress to be treasured.

Persuade him to have a small sketch book with him at all times, to be filled with a rough record of all his adventures and the drawn details of their settings.

IO. PRELIMINARY CONSIDERATIONS

THE EARLY SPONTANEOUS SCRIBBLES are indications of your child's innate sense of design. They should be kept and studied and from time to time compared with subsequent drawings as he advances.

These first scribbles of a very young child of three or four have almost no relation to the things he consciously remembers having seen. They are joyous emotional and physical outlets with no conscious strings. His early scribble is uninhibited, in contrast to the lack of adventurousness in the grown-up which causes him to follow a "style" to its usually dead end, and is only one of possibly hundreds of "designs" which flow naturally from a child. New ideas spring constantly and vitally to his mind and he does not become set in a mannered style of scribbling.

He should be encouraged to any artistic extravagance that may occur to him and his development not stunted by the adult's prejudices. However, in addition to the free scribble process he should be gently led to involve the conscious world of his daily life with this instinctive art flow.

Take the scribbles and play the following game with your child:

What animal, human or object shape can be discovered within that scribble. With him, turn the drawing on its sides and upside down. Invariably there lies within every scribble the elements of a recognizable representation of some object. Without changing the basic design, which must be considered as a spontaneous creation springing from intuitive sources and

[64]

therefore of value, either add a few features or stress part of the outline which will bring into being the representational form of an object or figure.

It is sort of a reverse procedure from that of the abstract artist. He takes an object and "abstracts" from it. That is, he takes from that object the elements of shape and design which he considers important and in the process loses some of the realistic aspects of the original object.

In our game we begin with the abstraction and return in some measure to the realistic. The pleasure of the game is a stimulant to the things to be learned from the transition. In the next chapter are a few examples of the procedure.

Get him to tell you how he felt when he made that scribble. Does it mean anger or pleasure; does it signify anything to him in story form? This will stimulate him to think in more related terms and his imagination will be tied in with his hitherto vague drawings.

II. PLAY

IT IS OF THE UTMOST IMPORTANCE that the urge to "play," a form of free expression in all children, be integrated with the art expression urged upon a child. Play is so natural and "unlearned" a part of a child's development process that it partakes of the very essence of art expression, inasmuch as it springs from sources of energy that seek an outlet and find expression in terms of symbols and make-believe.

Since all drawing and painting is a process of translating into symbols and simulations the things we see and feel, the play character of drawing and painting is easily suggestable to a child.

Herbert Read, the art critic, quotes in his *Education Through Art* from Froebel, "play is the highest expression of human development in the child, for it alone is the free expression of what is in a child's soul. It is the purest and most spiritual product of the child, and at the same time it is a type and copy of human life at all its stages and in all relations." The integration of the play instinct with art expression must be accomplished by subtle means.

Public schools have always missed out in this integrating process by the failure to realize the stimulus involved. Art classes, except in the kindergarten stages, are made into study courses, weighted down with exams and grades, a procedure always loaded with ominous portent for a child. The play character of art is gone and the work element stressed, with the menace of the monthly report card rating in "art" an additional deterrent to spontaneity.

[66]

Schools may have their problems in overcoming this blighted procedure but at home the art play game can be freely indulged.

The physical exercise play of children must not be invaded to be replaced by drawing and painting, for physical energy releases are indispensable, but relaxed play with toy soldiers and trains can be most profitably replaced with crayons and paints. The child's natural interest in soldiers and trains can be exercised graphically and the game becomes doubly interesting to him if cleverly directed.

WRIGGLY LINE GAME

A stimulating creative game is that of the "wriggly line drawing." Make a spontaneous, unplanned scrawl on the paper and give the child the problem of making a figure or animal using the line as a base unchanged but with any amount of additions. Then have him make the scrawl for you to work on. The inventiveness and ingenuity brought into play by the "wriggly game" added to the fun, make for a most valuable exercise, as may be seen by the examples shown on the pages following.

WRIGGLY LINE GAMES

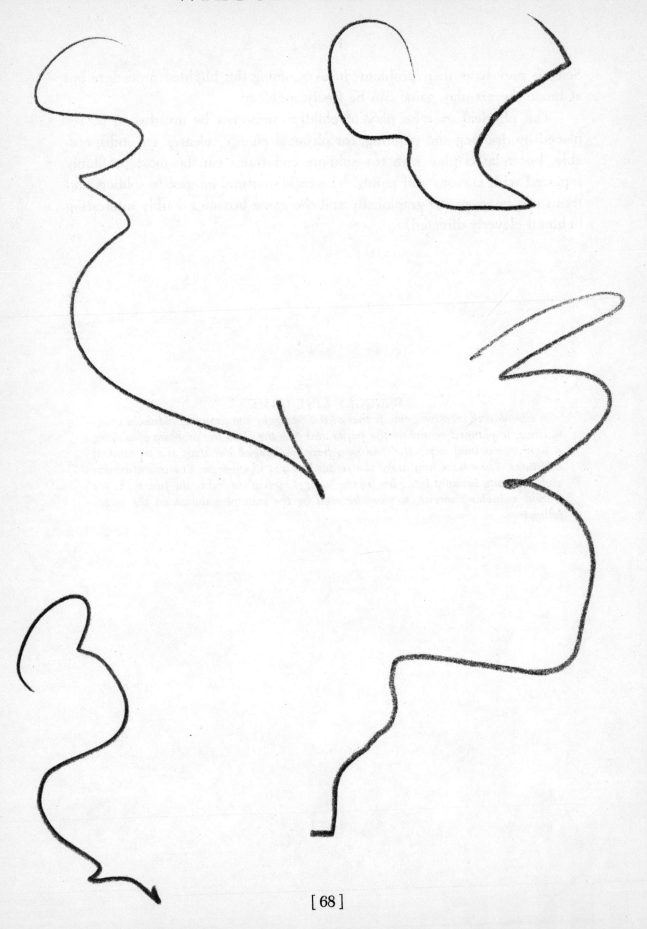

The play involved in drawing a line from number to number in this drawing also stimulates the ability to draw. You can make these puzzle figures easily by tracing any figure from a magazine in closely spaced numbers.

[70]

BLOT GAME

Another creative game calculated to stimulate an interest in design is the "blot game."

A sheet of paper is first folded in two and then the sheet is opened out.

With a dripping wet brush a blot design is made on one side of the line of the fold.

The paper is then folded on the crease line again and the still wet blot will reproduce itself on the opposite side of the crease, forming a balanced design.

[71]

12. DEXTERITY
AND CONSISTENCY

DRAWINGS AND PAINTINGS by young children represent vision at its most unadulterated purity, unspoiled by technical tricks which adults acquire to the inevitable detriment of valid vision.

Were it not for a lack of manual dexterity and complete muscular control, which come only with long practice, this clear, simple vision would always get fuller expression in a child, for there is no mental restraint or conscious inhibition, as yet, to hamper him.

Another deterrent to complete expression of vision is a capriciousness which tends to make children wander in their original purpose and allows vagaries unrelated to the original theme to enter and sometimes destroy the strength or simplicity of the work.

You must endeavor to direct the purposeful completion of the theme originally chosen by first eliciting the "story" the child has conceived for execution and then recalling that theme to the not-always-constant mind of the child. Consistency in the carrying out of the project, once begun, is important.

Dexterity: manual dexterity can be acquired by simple exercises with a pencil. As a sort of game-project the following rhythm patterns should be practiced.

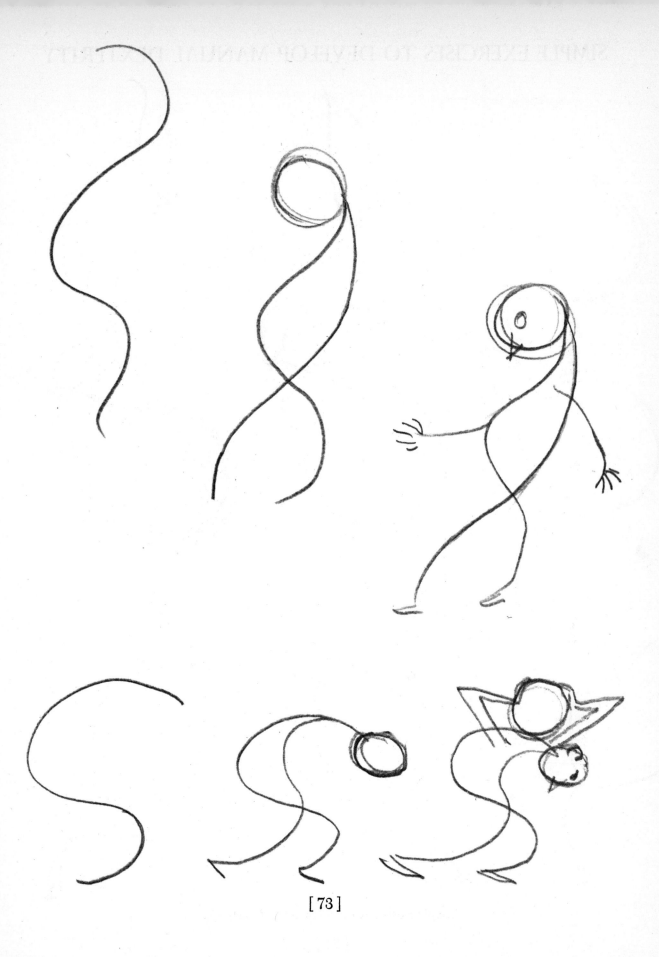

SIMPLE EXERCISES TO DEVELOP MANUAL DEXTERITY

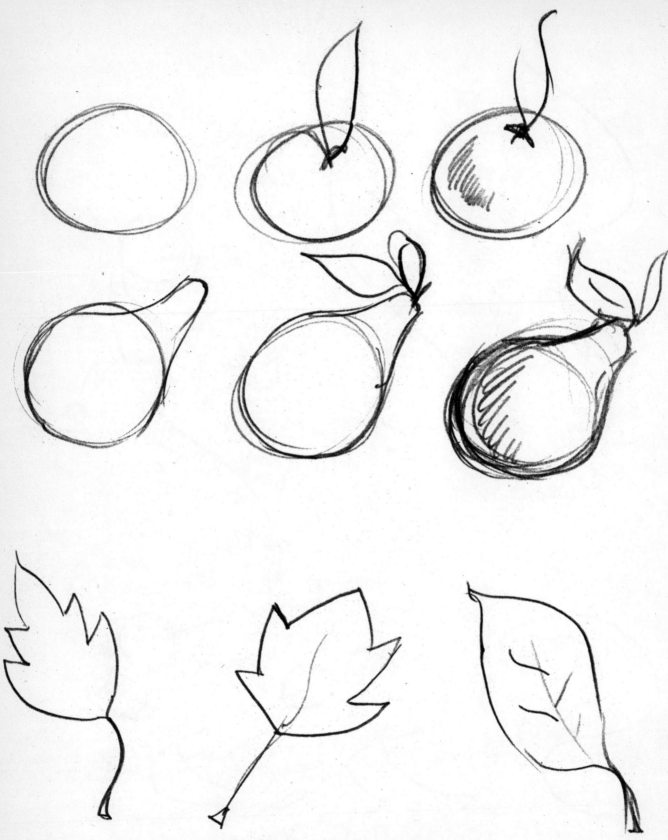

Simple exercises to develop manual dexterity.

13. CRITICISM

WHEN YOU GIVE A SIMPLE PROBLEM in drawing to your child your general criticism should be based on the following considerations:

1. How interested was he in the object and the problem?
2. How much ingenuity and imagination did he bring to the drawing?
3. How closely did he emulate the appearance of the object?

The last should be the least important consideration, providing that he scored high on the first two points.

As was stressed in previous pages of this book, the exact simulation of an object is far less important than is a unique viewpoint and imagination and intensity of observation. A reasonable facsimile plus a valid emotion is worth far more than a faithful representation without any emotional content.

The first consideration, that of interest, calls for a job on your part. You must so present the problem to the child that you will awaken in him a purposeful approach. If you want him to draw an apple, accompany the request that he draw it with a preamble which will make the apple an object of importance and even romance. A few words signifying your own wonder at nature's ingenuity in creating a thing of such beauty and usefulness might serve to stimulate his impressionable mind. The story of Adam and Eve, or William Tell, or Newton and the apple will evoke a romantic attitude and consequently localize his interest in the apple. Such obvious examples of relat-

The girl in this picture painted by an adolescent boy does not resemble any of his playmates nor does it resemble his mother. The saccharine sweetness of line and color are his conception of the ideal feminine figure.

The apparently privileged child who painted this picture was the son of selfish parents; his unconscious resentment of their treatment is shown in this drawing of a Christmas tree with a witch-like figure on top of the tree which has strings tied to all his gifts and snatches them out of his reach.

ing a story to an inanimate object for the purpose of stimulating interest are applicable to almost any object.

Having awakened an interest in the object itself, it becomes necessary to give purpose to the drawing or painting of that object. The bribe of possession is, of course, a basic purpose giver. However, it must be made clear that the drawing of the object is its own reward. This is partially achieved by ultimate praise of the work but the beginning stimulant must be given by stressing the importance of the drawing.

One of the most compelling impulses in a child is the desire to emulate adult activities. He will be much impressed with the importance of drawing if you do it also, for even though the actions of adults are often incomprehensible to a child, they always seem of great importance to him.

Having romanced about the object, begun to draw it yourself and supplied him with materials to do likewise, he cannot help applying himself with interest to the task. The amount of interest evoked can be judged from his application and results, and should serve to guide you in stimulating him for the next problem in drawing.

The second consideration is the amount of ingenuity and imagination he brought to the drawing. In judging the factors a generalization will serve to cover the approach.

How "original" is the style of his line or color? Is it a stereotyped vision set by the already ruinous influences of school formula drawing or dime store "paint books" or is it the unspoiled vision of a fresh viewpoint?

How much ingenuity does it show? How well did he translate to two dimensional language the three dimensions of the object? How well did he employ the pencil or crayon or brush? In examining these details the important points of judgment are not the expertness of the use of the materials, which naturally the child cannot automatically possess, but rather the amount of inventiveness and adaptability he showed in using the relatively unfamiliar tools.

When analyzing the drawings made by your child two purposes must be borne in mind. One is what the drawing indicates to you as to the condition and type of mind your child has. This does not mean that you are called upon to be an amateur child psychologist nor are you expected to treat any neurosis you think you discover. It is merely with the intention of understanding him and his problems in a general parental way that the character analysis to be discovered from his drawings should be used.

The second purpose in examining the drawing is for the purpose of seeking constructive critical points.

The drawings should be analyzed for:

1. Sureness and quality of his lines.
2. General proportions.
3. An understanding of elements of perspective.
4. A feeling for composition.
5. Color quality.
6. An understanding of light, its source and shadows and their cause.
7. Subject matter and mood.

These elements of a drawing or painting will be dealt with in later chapters in some detail to aid in your understanding of the problems involved and give you a basis for sound criticism of his work.

I4. LEARNING BY DOING

FOR CHILDREN words only take on meaning when they assume visual form in terms of action or example. Teachers who use the verbal instruction method only are usually amazed to find that the points of their lecture least relevant and important are remembered only because these points evoked some sharp visual image. Most children will recall Peter Stuyvesant, for instance, long after they have forgotten more significant characters, due to his dramatic and picturesque wooden leg. A picture has been formed and impressed itself permanently.

An even more effective teaching method is "doing." A point of instruction which requires the making of a graph or a design will be registered far more securely in the child's mind than will a lesson read or told. When called upon to use the skill of his hands, the child shares creatively in study, bearing out the teachings of John Dewey that instruction through direct experience is best.

Begin the process of "learning by doing" with a simple bribe. Offer an apple or a stick of candy in exchange for a drawing of that apple or candy. The simple shape and the bright color present an easy challenge but a good test of eye and hand aptitude. A series of such tests with all the available easy objects should fix the drawing habit and start the training of eye and hand dexterity necessary to supplement natural vision and ability. At the same time, make a drawing of the object yourself, not in a spirit of competition but as a means of knowing from first-hand experience what problems your child faces.

If you keep up with him in these tests, you will surprise yourself with the pleasure and interest you will develop in the process of drawing. You may also surprise yourself with the springs of latent ability you tap in yourself.

Compare with your child the drawings you each make and such criticism as you feel inclined to make of his drawing will be tempered with respect for the problems involved in the subject as you encountered them.

The communion established by sharing these problems will lack the air of patronage involved in most other attempts to share in a child's play or study. In most cases his drawing will be on a plane of equality with yours, if you are "untrained." His ego will not suffer and his competitive spirit will be stimulated in a healthy fashion.

You, on the other hand, may be piqued at what you consider a shocking lack of obvious superiority over your infant, a superiority which you have in all other fields.

His drawing will usually have a freshness and lack of inhibition not to be found in yours even though your manual control may produce a more skillful approximation of the contours and forms.

SIMPLE EXERCISES INVOLVING THE BASIC FORMS — CIRCLE, SQUARE AND TRIANGLE

Any four-year-old child can draw a square or a circle in such a way that everyone will know what is intended.

The next step is to add such detail to that circle or square as to give it directed meaning.

The addition of a stem to the circle will convey the symbol of an apple and carry along with that first literal symbol a sense of success to the child which will stimulate further attempts.

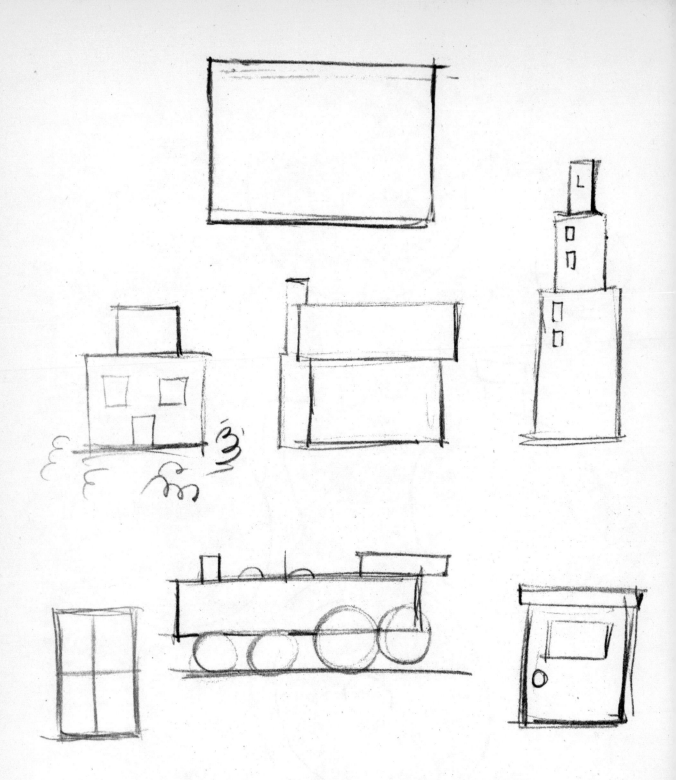

Some *windows* to his square will symbolize a house and the child's first approximation of that important prop to his sense of security is an accomplishment equal
in satisfaction to what you would feel if you built a real house with your own hands.

[82]

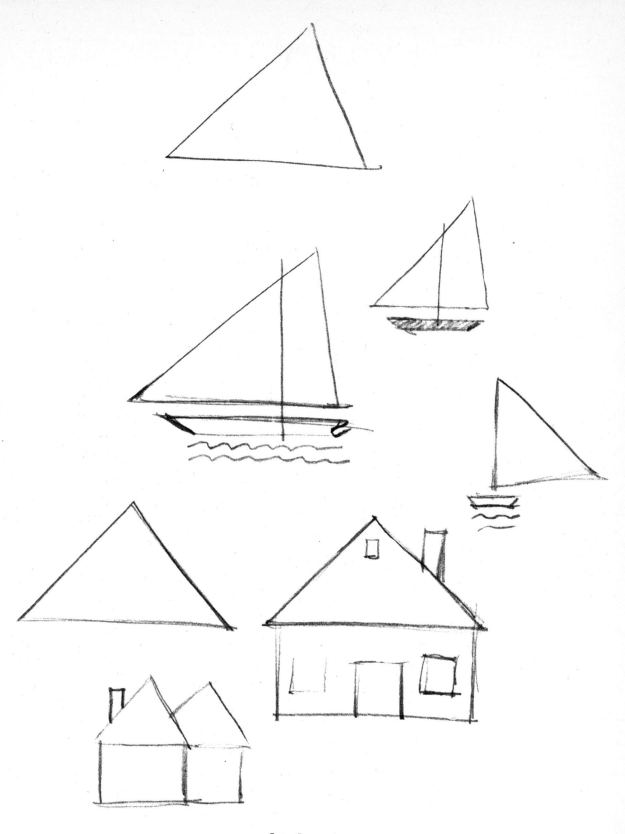

Along with the free-play art, which allows for uncurbed experiment and imagination, he should be encouraged to practice the expression of some concrete fact, that of a tangible object, expressible in terms of a developed circle or square and their variations — the sphere, cube, oblong and oval.

[85]

DEVELOPING THE FIGURE DRAWING

Having begun to indicate the figure or object by a few familiar features, ask the child to develop the idea. It would be an excellent plan to use transparent paper to trace the original scribble design and then proceed with the development on the tracing.

Try to point out how the resultant figure or object drawing came from the first scribble and that your child really "created."

The term "created" will not mean anything to him unless it is translated into terms understandable to his ego and you may be sure that ego is ever present and always craving nourishment.

Point out to him that he "made" that animal or object by "himself" out of nothing—that it is "his."

It is very important to the success of the game and his own natural creative urge that he recognizes the value of his accomplishment.

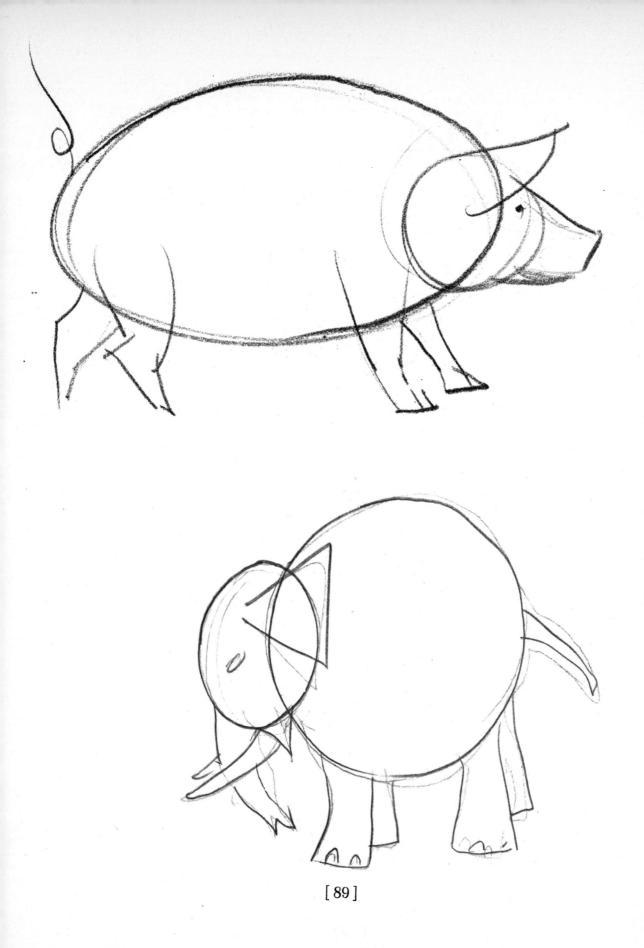

[89]

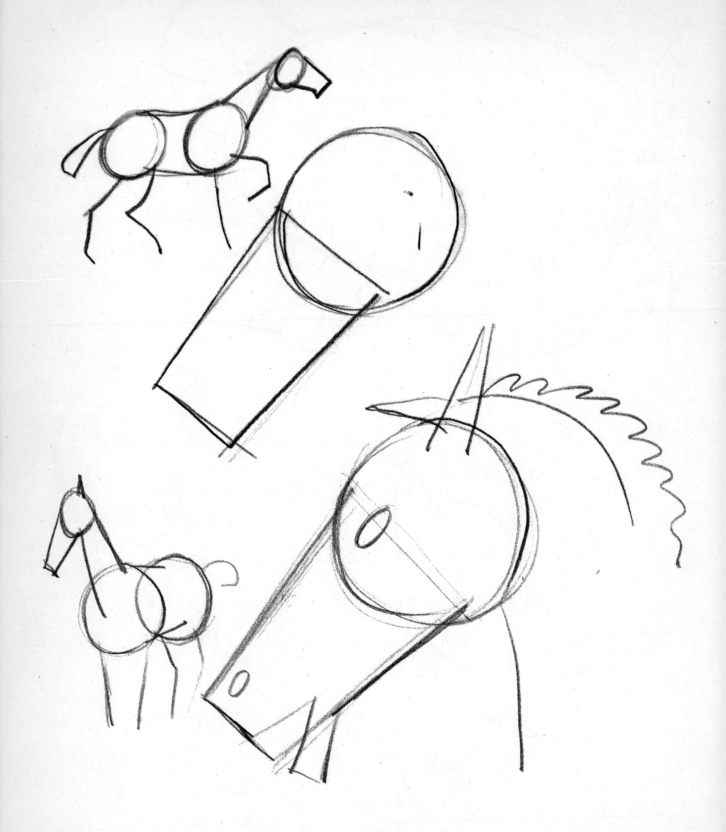

*An unusually simple, yet dynamic, depiction of a New York traffic police-
man by a six-year-old boy.*

15. LET HIM DO IT HIS WAY

THE BEST FORM OF EDUCATION lies in giving the best possible opportunity for self development. You must make sure that the three major ingredients for creative growth are allowed to flourish unhindered and only guided occasionally when the direction taken is obviously wrong. The three major ingredients are *imagination, courage* and *vision*.

Imagination is the forerunner of future experience, based on past experience and with spice of the unreal mixed with the real. The wilder and freer the imagination the richer the creation will be.

Courage must accompany imagination to widen its scope and free the child from fear of expressing his thoughts.

Vision is the ability to "see" things as they are and to visualize things we dream. We all have it and the child often has it in greater degree and clarity than adults. Children must be permitted to express these three parts of the creative whole in their own manner and in their chosen language.

If the child insists on making a horse green, let him; your function as a teacher would be solely to show him that green may be made with yellow and blue pigment.

Encourage fearless exploration. Teach him to see cause and effect but let him find the Q.E.D. himself and it will not necessarily be the same solution as yours. Do not force your mental heirlooms on him. Let him do it *his* way.

[93]

*Commonplace objects make an uncommonly interesting arrangement in the
work of this thirteen-year-old American girl.*

16. DRAWING OBJECTS

A HOUSE to the young child presents a very different visual experience than does the same house to an adult. The adult, when he looks at the front of a house, brings to the image reflected on his retina a large supplementary store of *a priori* knowledge. He has been around the corner and seen the four sides of the house. He knows that it has bulk and great weight and is supported by a foundation and strong beams. He knows something of the texture of the materials used in building it. His learning evokes the historic period of its architecture. He gauges from the probable cost the class and wealth of its builder and owner.

All these and many more factors condition the adult eye to an unconscious translation of the simple linear image of the house thrown on his retina to a highly complex picture and it is that picture that he "sees."

On the other hand, the eye of the child, knowing nothing of the above ramifications "sees" with an innocent directness. The word "house" lacks the structural implications to a child which are obvious to an adult. In regarding it as an object he has little or no realization of its three-dimensional bulk. The building materials and their weight and texture have no part in his visual analysis. What is uppermost in his mind and obvious in his visual interpretation is the meaning of "house" to him, its implications as a haven of security or the cold austerity of someone else's house, the fearful importance of the school building or the impersonal vague loom of the apartment building down the street. His is never an objective viewpoint because of the intense personalization of his attitudes.

Added to his emotional approach to "house" is his naïve sense of perception, unburdened by experience. He has probably never walked around all four sides of the house to be drawn. He has certainly had limited experience in judging distances and measurements. He draws what he thinks he sees without established conventions to guide him.

Problems of perspective are handled without restraint and the results are usually not sound from the viewpoint of an engineer or architect since the basic laws of physics are often violated. He does not necessarily, however, violate the laws of art (a contradiction in terms) since the artist does not copy nature and objects but rather interprets them in terms of their meaning to him.

A remarkably free delineation of an apartment house by a seven-year-old.
Perhaps the trees symbolize a desire to escape from the city streets.

A weird but beautifully spaced concept of school, street and fellow students. The vague character of the adjacent building—notice the flying window—indicates the relative importance of school in this young artist's life.

17. SUBJECT MATTER

A CHILD'S DAY is full of small adventures, though they seem very big to him. They, compositely, are the experiences which his environment contributes to the molding of his character and mind. Except for certain hereditary potentials these experiences are the sole source of mental growth.

It is from these experiences that one should draw the subject matter for his art endeavors. The experiences are not only concrete ones in terms of events and actions. They are also made up of his dreams, inner reactions and unconscious desires. These are stimulated by the contacts and events of his daily experiences and crystalize into mental images quite different from the simple, outer facts of the experiences.

If a child can be stimulated to draw and paint these mental images he will make most fascinating pictures. Most children can be stimulated to put on paper what they think and feel about the commonplace events of their lives. The results are rarely commonplace. A passing fire engine, a visit to the dentist, or a baseball game are fraught with enormous drama and the drawing suggested by such scenes will inevitably contain the element of drama they feel.

Drawings related to the subjects studied in school are inevitably more directly felt and understood than are newly introduced, strange themes. When the child is persuaded to draw events or subjects from his school day it takes on a little of the character of "playing school," popular with most children.

This simple but arresting still life by a talented thirteen-year-old shows remarkable facility in handling everyday objects in a dynamic composition.

18. SELECTION

IN MAKING A PICTURE OF AN OBJECT a young child need not be told that he is not a photographer and that rigid selection must be made from the infinite mass of factual detail present in every object whether a leaf or a chair. The young child does not think in terms of the need for economy but his unencumbered mind expresses his impression of the object rather than the visual facts exhaustively examined.

As the child grows older, the mass of knowledge regarding objects, their structure, source, texture and manufacturing process leads him to attempt exact simulation. Added to the aforementioned knowledge is his increasing self-consciousness and the fear of being "different" which leads him to try even more to be "naturalistic."

Older students of drawing must have impressed upon them the need to retain and stress their *impression* rather than the cold facts of what they see. An exercise in stimulating this is to limit the older child in time given to make a drawing of an object. Realizing the need for economy of effort he will be forced to selectivity. He will stress contour of the form rather than surface details, essence of a movement rather than the mechanical details of articulation in moving forms.

[101]

Exercises repeating a theme from many angles.
Very good practice for developing observation and dexterity.

[102]

19. REPETITION

IT IS NOT IMPORTANT that in his subsequent painting your child be expected to remember exactly "how" he was told to correct the proportions or color or perspective. More important is to impress him as to "why" he must seek certain harmonies.

Each picture he draws will present a quite different problem and spring from different sources of his experience. Previous "know how" is not always applicable. New art experiences call for solutions not previously knowable. Your cooperative criticism will be required, based on each new venture and it will be of profit to you as well as to the child. He must not strain to remember how he did that previous bit of painting that won your approval, for he might easily fall into clichés of expression in order to repeat that approval. In addition to the danger of falling into dull repetition to win approval, it may retard his natural adventurousness, for he is in a process of constant growth and every hour he is a different child from the one he was the previous hour, with different problems and different solutions.

An extraordinary evocation of the fear caused a ten-year-old by the long stair-cases and gloomy corridors of his school.

2O. MEMORY PICTURES

MEMORY is a splendid source of pictures. You often hear people refer to a "photographic" memory as a rarity and it is fortunate for art that this is so.

Most of us have memories of things seen and done which are a composite of those things and deeds plus our moods and imaginations, blurred or enriched by intervening time.

A child sees objects and remembers them very sharply. These things seen are not registered on jaded senses but on very fresh eager ones stimulated by an insatiable curiosity.

Added to the sharp memory of the thing is the invariable factor of some strong emotional response, desire for the thing seen, fear of it, love for it, but only rarely indifference to it.

It is inevitable that he will call upon the remembrances of things seen and done as subject matter for drawings, once he has passed from the unconscious scribble state to representational drawing.

As a stimulant to his impressionable vision, find out what has interested him most at kindergarten or at the circus or in the street and take him again to see these things to add to his most interesting visual experiences.

Afterwards, have him draw from memory. You will notice that the details have very little to do with his viewpoint. Some salient feature which you perhaps will have considered unimportant will have impressed itself upon him and he will stress it in his drawing. Question his reasons before discouraging his preoccupation with those seemingly irrelevant features, for some strong emotional response is involved and it is in the things most emotionally felt that his talents will show.

[105]

An "unseen drawing," made by looking only at the objects in the room and not at the paper. It shows good coordination between hand and eye.

2I. UNSEEN DRAWING

SUGGEST THE FOLLOWING EXERCISE as an excellent form of training hand and eye coordination. Set up a simple still life, perhaps a bowl of fruit or a pitcher and a glass. Have the child draw looking only at the still life and not down at the paper. The results will perhaps be ludicrous at first but with practice an amazing amount of dexterity will develop in doing these "unseen drawings."

Another excellent training for the power of observation and coordination is to look long at the still life set-up—say three minutes, without drawing, then turn away and draw from what you observed without looking at the subject.

Both these exercises are highly effective in preventing a slavish attempt to copy exactly the unimportant details but rather to register the essentials. These two methods of exercise are entirely different in their value. The first, that of not looking at the drawing, will be aimed solely at developing hand and eye coordination. The second, study of the object and then drawing it without further reference to it, produces a strong sense of observation combined with discrimination as to essence.

A remarkable "inner view" picture by a thirteen-year-old boy.

22. INNER VIEW PICTURES

A SOURCE OF VISION and a consequent source of pictures is the inventive mind supplemented by what may be called the intuitive eye. The process of evoking these "inner views" can best be demonstrated by immediate experiment.

Relax and close your eyes and dismiss as much of the "thinking" process as you can from your mind. Shapes of color and light slowly form and shift about and develop. Now study these ephemeral shapes and memorize their color and character. Freely and swiftly transfer these memories into paint and line on your paper. Have the child do the same thing and compare and discuss the impressions and results.

Salvadore Dali, the surrealist, in his autobiography tells how, as a child, he would press his closed lids with his fingers until his eyes popped inwardly in order to see the "spots" of design flare on his tortured retina.

We hardly advocate such stringent methods for evoking pictures but milder efforts in the same direction will produce most interesting results and the drawings of these inner views make fascinating designs.

Another way of evoking "spots" is to close the lids and stare hard at an electric bulb. The forms which move on the retina are living designs, original and transient as those made in a kaleidoscope.

An apple close to the eye is larger than an elephant in the distance and still larger than a house or mountains further away.

23. PERSPECTIVE AND PROPORTION

NOTICE that in drawings or paintings by children of from four to six the pattern is usually flat. They do not see in terms of a third dimension.

Proportion is mostly a matter of emphasis to the child—that is, the figure or thing considered most important to him is enlarged in relation to other things with no regard for the relative distances from the eye or for the basic differences in dimension.

This does not reflect on the child's intelligence, for until early in the Italian Renaissance perspective drawing was an unknown science and much splendid art of many countries had only a two-dimensional character with background and foreground of equal value and often equal size with no regard for actual proportions and diminishing perspective.

A simple explanation of the principle of optics involved—that an object at a greater distance from the eye "appears" smaller than an object at close range will start your child observing this phenomenon and the result in his learning to put things in their proper space relation.

The distortion of proportion in drawings by young children will tend to decrease as the child grows older and he draws more of what he "sees" and less of what he "knows."

Distorted proportion may often have a very real, but unconscious, reason for being. The importance of one part of a figure in relation to another in the child's mind may cause the stress and preoccupation with that part which leads to distorted proportion.

Excessive criticism of this distortion will not accomplish any valuable end and only when the child is old enough to understand the value of true proportion and has passed the danger of discouragement through being convinced of his incompetence is it advisable to insist on correction of distortion.

[111]

24. MATCHSTICK MEN

THE "MATCHSTICK MAN" is the primitive drawing simplification common to all peoples, young and old. It is by no means an indication of an inability to draw "properly." On the contrary, it represents the first step in artistic translation from the real and representational to the symbolic and abstract. In essence matchstick men are what is most devoutly sought by the artist, the expression of form in terms of symbol and line both non-existent in nature and strictly within the province of the artist.

When your child starts to make them, as he inevitably will, direct him into paths of creative development by suggesting that the figure "do" things and that, along with being the "essence of man," the figure perform the essence of an action.

Actually to see the human figure in terms of a matchstick man is to have reached a degree of artistic sophistication, for all good drawing is an approximation and involves the use of symbols rather than attempt at photographic representation. The matchstick is to drawing what the wire armature is to sculpture. It represents the raw essence of human design.

To the child such symbols convey all that he feels necessary to imply a man's figure. To the adult it usually seems an inadequate or a funny cartoon.

In this simple example it can be demonstrated that the child's vision and reason is basically "better" than a grownup's for purposes of direct artistic expression.

Matchstick figures are, of course, not an end in themselves, though they have been used with telling effect from time to time. They are, however, good practice for action sketches where speed is required to catch a fleeting movement. They are also a good "hanger" upon which may be placed the details of more solid anatomy.

[113]

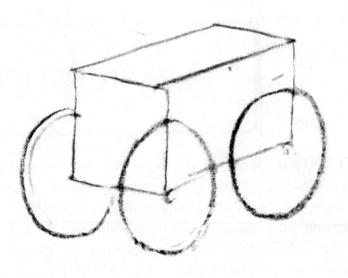

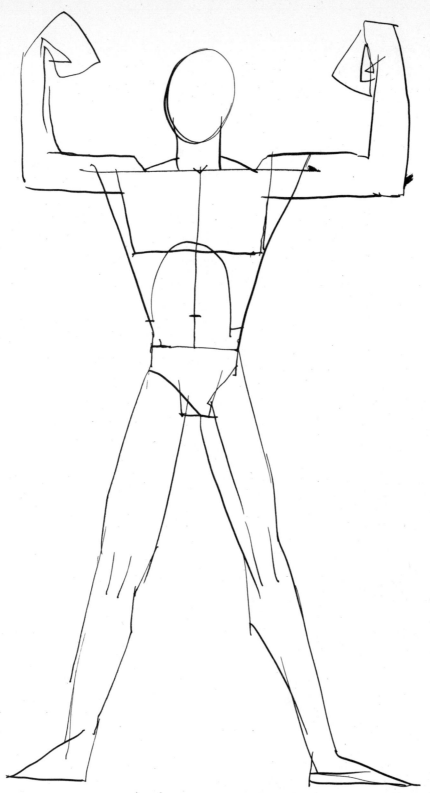

The next step from matchstick figures is the two-dimensional design figure in which the forms of the body are reduced to simple geometric elements.

[117]

THESE FIGURE DRAWINGS BY 6- AND 7-YEAR-OLD CHILDREN *show*
a high degree of powers of observation in spite of distortion and over-simplification.
They represent the truth as the child sees it.

THE FIGURE *in relation to trees, houses and other figures.*

PICASSO

The Picasso head at the left is a study in essential expression and these children's drawings partake of that same essential character.

[122]

THESE ANCIENT PRIMITIVE FIGURES *are remarkably parallel to the preceding figure drawings by today's children.*

Eleventh Century carved figures and animals, a charmingly simplified style, childlike but not childish.

[124]

CONVENTIONALIZED FIGURE

A convention or style of representation of the human figure was conceived by some unknown artist of ancient Egypt and it was accepted as the pattern for most Egyptian figure drawings and carvings.

Unfamiliar with the laws of perspective or proportion, this early artist invented a method of suggesting bulk and three dimensions.

His relatively naive viewpoint along with that of his contemporary artists succeeded in evoking a charming and decorative concept, born of the innocent eye and similar to that of a child.

25. COLOR

YOUR YOUNG CHILD reacts to color in quite a different fashion from you. His tastes in color are not affected by the many considerations which have long since tempered any primitive color sense you possessed to begin with.

In adults there creep in such insidious factors as a need for quiet, dignity, repressing of emotion, blending for "good taste" and fashions in color. Inevitably these considerations affect our choices of color, along with many other factors of both conscious and unconscious sources which accumulate during the process of compromising our urges and accommodating them to society.

Your child is a creature of moods in his color sense. His choices of color, though sometimes pure vagaries on his part, are often clearly to be linked with the state of his well being. Researches have shown that the choice of yellow indicates gaiety, blue anxiety, red excitement. Your child will choose sombre colors when depressed, light colors when happy.

Children like to use the raw colors as they come from the little cups or tubes. They rarely bother with mixing or tinting when they first begin to splash it on paper.

As they grow older and have learned to channelize their exuberance somewhat, it is well to give them a few directions in the mixing of colors to produce other colors, blends and tints.

This abstraction by an exceptionally artistic 7-year-old girl is distinguished by an unusual choice of colors and an instinctive feeling for design.

A ten-year-old boy who lives in one of the most crowded areas of lower Manhattan expressed his longing for open spaces in this painting. His imagination created a realistic picture of a Western ranch, but the earth is painted the dirty color of the slums with which he is familiar.

COLOR

Point out that invariably the mixture of:

yellow and blue makes green

yellow and red makes orange

red and blue makes purple

that red, yellow and blue mixed make brown

that white added to any color gives a tint of that basic color
and varies with the quantity of white added

that tints of varying strength may also be attained by diluting
the pigment with water

that black and white makes grey.

There are innumerable combinations of colors, tints and blends available to the adventurous mixer and entirely dependent on the amount and intensity of each ingredient color.

Encourage boldness and experimentation in your young colorist. He has it innately, unless curbed by dull examples or restraint.

A *child* rarely thinks in terms of "composition" and his arrangement of forms is usually entirely haphazard and accidental.

A *few* pointers on balance and "right" placement of the subject within the given space, based on your own adult concepts, will aid him in thinking in terms of composition instead of relying on pure intuition.

26. COMPOSITION

OBJECTS IN NATURE are not faced with the same problems as the artist in drawing them. He must put his drawing in an arbitrary space set by the limits of his paper. He must harness the wild profusion, the lack of selectivity, that differentiates nature from the artist. He must put what he does within a "frame."

Whether the drawing contains one object or a group of objects, the placing of the drawn area as related to the "empty" area is as much a part of the artistic, aesthetic problem as is the drawn part itself.

The drawing plus the spacing are what is called the "composition." There are no set rules for composition any more than there are set rules for how to draw or paint any given object. Elements of intuition are as important as elements of reason. "Feeling" is as much a factor as knowing. A combination of the two will make a "right" composition.

There are, however, certain composition structures and arrangements which have a greater truth quality than others because they are closer to the physical laws—laws of gravity, stress and strain, and balance.

The average eye is accustomed to a general orderliness ruled by these physical laws and any disarrangement calls for adjustments in taste habits not easily accomplished.

Distribution of the weights and quantities of objects in a composition based on "orderliness" makes for sound conventional composition. Obviously, overbalance on one side of a given area is not "good" composition any more than if you were stowing cargo in the hold of a ship in such a manner. On the other hand, exact mathematical balance of forms in a composition makes for dullness.

What should be sought is that nice balance which will not keel over nor ride dully or heavily but rather, to continue to use the nautical simile, tack and fill with the winds of the picture problem.

Another dynamic composition. This one is based on a central figure design with a circle of figures in various rhythmic poses calculated to give a maximum of movement and counter-movement yet always returning to the center.

Composition done with a strong feeling for the dramatic. The mood was materially aided by the use of diagonal lines offset by the graceful arch as a background to the austere verticals of the chair and figures.

Non-objective "finger painting" made by a four-year-old boy who was obviously obeying motor and emotional impulses of which he could not possibly be conscious.

27. NON-OBJECTIVE ART AND COLOR
By Dr. S. Z. Orgel

ANY ATTEMPT to understand the emotional qualities inherent in the individual child artist's painting of non-objective art must be limited to and deduced from the colors used, the way they are used, their arrangement, and the forms and pattern produced by their use. All of these must have a symbolic meaning and value to the child which depict his inner emotional feeling of a positive or negative nature.

At exhibitions reviewing the life works of artists, we frequently notice that during certain periods of the artist's evolution, his painting has been done predominantly in one color. Frequently the critics in attempting to understand the artist from his work have tried to make an analysis of these periods by virtue of the dominant color used in the painting. Thus we have been told that this denotes the artist's "Blue Period," this his "Red Period," and so on. These colors are thus meant to convey to the uninitiated the supposed emotional state of the artist during the period in which these colors dominated his paintings. The "Blue Period" was supposed to be associated with a depressed mood; the "Red Period" with a hypomanic or manic mood. In these cases, color alone was utilized as the diagnostic feature. We can only doubt the validity of such a hasty conclusion. These moods, as indicated by the number of paintings done therein, must have been of a prolonged duration and must of necessity have evidenced themselves by other indications in the paintings.

[133]

Just as in mental disease, there is no monomania, so too in Art the mood cannot limit itself merely to the color used and to nothing else. Since the color seems to be the main evidence upon which the diagnosis of the type of mood was based, we can but state that such an interpretation is erroneous. A close study of these "periods" in the lives of some artists shows that during these periods the only constant and monotonous characteristic of the painting was the color used. The productivity has usually been the same regardless of a supposed "depressed" or "manic" phase. The objects utilized are of the form and type usually used by the artist and the production has definite artistic merit. Depressions or manic phases when they occur in an individual, be he artist or not, produce a similar effect that permeates his entire personality.

The depressed artist would produce but few, if any, paintings; his technique would be labored, stilted and rigid. His forms would be small, tight and poorly formed and frequently incomplete. His pattern would be repetitious and would show little if any ingenuity. We should be hard put to recognize the painting as the work of an artist and might indeed believe, if we were not told differently, that it was the work of a child.

The manic artist's production would be quite different from the above description. He would produce many paintings but none, if any, would be complete. Most of the canvases would have but a stroke or two of bright color anywhere on the canvas. His technique would be free and florid, he would have difficulty in completing a form and such a form would be large and poorly formed. He would completely lack the patience necessary to complete a form on the complete canvas. Both these periods carry with them a lack of ability to concentrate. In one, the thoughts and ideas are labored and slow or absent. In the other, they are flighty and tumble over one another without direction.

In the milder forms of the psychosis in which these two major states are not too pronounced, we frequently find that when given access to paints, patients will readily and willingly express themselves in color and form. The colors and forms used will usually run parallel to the type of severity of the illness, the mood of the patient and his thoughts.

Severely depressed psychotic patients are usually found to use predominently such colors as dark blue, black or grey. The forms will be small and placed low in the painting as if in the ground and will consist of circles or squares with some contained object symbolic of the womb or death. They may also assume the shape of hills symbolizing breasts. As the depression begins to lift, other warmer and less morbid colors are utilized and the dark browns, umbers, and purples begin to appear. The forms become large, looser, less rigid in shape and are above ground. Hills, large circles, houses and boxes usually predominate. As they approach normalcy, we find the greens, light blues, pinks and violets used freely. The forms take on more normal shapes and tend to be open and paint upward and outward, thus symbolizing a rebirth and a return to life and love. Should this go into a hypo-manic or manic phase, the bright and more violent colors come into use, such as bright reds and yellows. In this state the artist shows an excessive flight of his emotion with a complete inability to form a pattern. His shapes are form-less; there is no order or style.

It is the presence of these characteristics in the painting of psychotics that has helped the psychiatrist to get a better understanding of the patient's mood, its variations, its progress or regression. Painting thus forms a valu-able diagnostic, prognostic and therapeutic aid in the treatment of the mentally ill patient.

Utilizing the above as a basis, I have attempted to interpret some of the non-objective paintings of these children. It is well to keep in mind that the adult when mentally ill regresses to the earlier periods of his childhood. He utilizes symbolisms that belongs to the period of childhood to which his evo-lution has regressed. Thus, we find that the symbols we consider abnormal for the adult are normal for the child.

NOTE: In the following pages the unsigned captions are the work of Arthur Zaidenberg; critical commentaries presenting the psychiatrist's interpretations are the work of Dr. S. Z. Orgel and are so labeled.

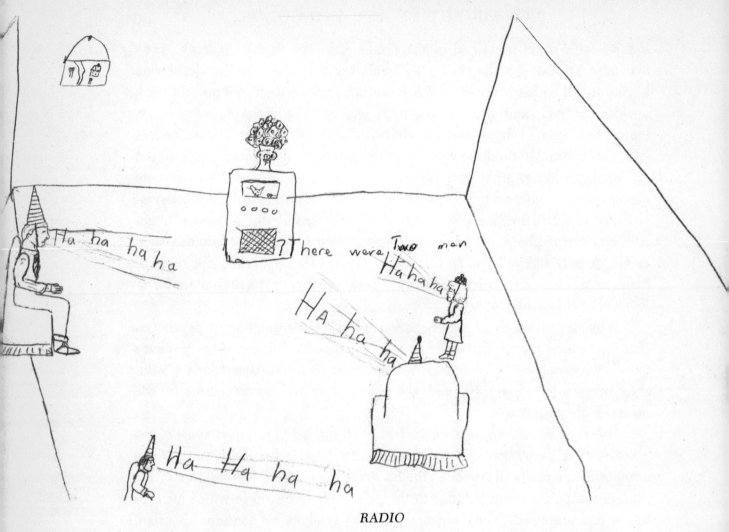

RADIO

This witty line drawing of a family around the radio is highly revealing of the boy's opinion of that family and of radio programs but it is even more revealing of the curious concept of proportion and perspective of the boy artist.

This charming farm scene by an eight-year-old boy is a truly original visualization. Notice the rich imaginative concepts of each of the separate farm areas, each enclosed and yet the whole picture well integrated. A. Z.

This crayon drawing by a boy eight years old would seem to indicate that he is a well-adjusted child who is accepted and loved by his family. The domestic scenes and those of the farm, as well as the brightly curtained windows all help to convey this feeling of warmth, safety and security.

The peacefulness of the people and animals in the scenes further express happiness and contentment.

This boy no doubt spends a major part of his summers on a farm where a happy and serene atmosphere prevails. Dr. S. Z. Orgel.

These two western story illustrations show the uninhibited bravery with which children attack a difficult subject which would stump the average adult.

This eight and one-half year old girl is a happy child who feels loved and secure at home and so can project herself into the joys of outdoor life and its activities. She shows a repetitiveness of pattern which would seem to symbolize that she has found an adequate means of solving her emotional situation at home and which has also proven useful and adequate in the outside world.

This little girl in her crayon drawing depicts outdoor scenes of a more adult type.
She evidently is a secure, expansive, outgoing child who receives a great amount of encouragement from the home. This seems to be mainly in the form of ice skating and dancing.
She evidently is a narcissistic and exhibitionist type of child who is being primed by her parents, especially mother, for the stage. DR. S. Z. ORGEL.

[140]

The upper drawing applies to a real incident and the lower to a fictional experience. Curiously enough the real incident has a dream quality and the imaginative subject is done in a realistic manner.

This flatly painted picture shows a fine feeling for design.
With no attempt at realism the girl, rope, tree, house, clouds, and the weird stars are "styled" to please the artist's whim. There is a rightness about the arrangement and the conventionalized forms which indicate thought combined with fine intuitive sense. A. Z.

This twelve-year-old girl expresses in her forms and colors the health and vigor of a pubescent girl who feels secure in her home and love life. There is evidently a great love for the outdoors and farm life and it is most likely associated with her whole-hearted acceptance of mother. DR. S. Z. ORGEL.

This crayon drawing by a 10½-year-old boy of men falling down stairs expresses an extremely aggressive and destructive urge in this child. The hate this child bears to his siblings is symbolized by the act of falling occurring within the confines of the home. Thus it carries with it the desire to have his parents punish the hated rival. The wish for the sibling's destruction (death wish) is also presented in the possibility of injury in the fall. If we consider the falling person a man, we may assume that it represents the child's death wish against father, thus enabling him to have mother as his sole possession (reactivated Oedipus complex). As long as the child expresses such wishes in drawing and fantasy, they are to be considered as normal. Dr. S. Z. Orgel.

So simply drawn as to appear at first glance to be a careless scribble, an impression of the "treeness" of a tree is conveyed compellingly and very satisfyingly.

If you still think it a careless scribble, try to draw a tree as freely. If you succeed, you've done well and if your child of that age can do that well he has more than enough "talent" to deserve encouragement. A. Z.

This drawing of a tree by a twelve-year-old girl conveys the impression that she is substantially a normal pubescent girl who is on the threshold of life and has accepted her femininity and is looking forward to going out in a new and greater life. The tree thereby representing life and the branches spreading upwards toward the sky symbolize her desire to leave the home and to go out into the world.

Such drawings with their freedom of line are usually the product of a child about to graduate from public school and who is joyfully looking forward to high school and college. DR. S. Z. ORGEL.

[144]

A common place incident with a dream quality. A child's dreams are crowded and often terrifying. Unable to recount them so that his fears may be treated psychiatrically, his drawings often give valuable clues to his obsessions and those dream fears. The old and accepted theory of "getting it out of the system" may work and the resultant drawings will surely be enormously interesting, coming as they do from deeply personal sources.

The mail truck is coming

catherine

ILLUSTRATIONS BY CHILDREN OF COMMONPLACE INCIDENTS

milk

TWO MOODY PICTURES OF UNCOMMON INCIDENTS

[149]

AN EXPLOSIVE PAINTING BY A TEMPERAMENTAL CHILD

28. THE PROBLEM CHILD

AS AN AID in treating "problem children," the school systems of many great cities have found drawing and painting of great value. Part of the Goodenough test involves drawing the figure of a man as a test of intelligence and adjustment. The trained child psychologist can determine much from such drawings, for a child often shows much less reticence in drawing than in telling of his problems. His responses to life about him, at school, play and home are strongly apparent in his drawings. But not only does his drawing serve as a guide to the psychologist in treating him but the exercise of drawing and painting itself has become recognized as a therapy of as yet unmeasured but obviously great value.

A layman should always be careful of conclusions he draws, based on an amateur's knowledge, of character judged from the drawings of these children. But parents troubled by certain behavior patterns of their child would do well to keep the drawings he makes and if a psychiatrist is consulted these drawings will be invaluable.

An adult searches for order in his intuitive scribbles.

29. CHILD NON-OBJECTIVE PAINTING

EVERYONE who is interested in art knows the controversy raging between those who paint or love non-objective art and those who demand more identifiable, natural symbols in their pictures.

Non-objective means exactly what the name implies—that no recognizable object is portrayed in the work, that the only considerations are form, line, color and space, irrespective of nameable "things." Whatever your tastes and prejudices are in that controversy, I have yet to find a child who was fazed by the problem or rather had even seen that there was a problem involved.

When asked, and indeed sometimes on his own, every child sees nothing strange or wrong in making blobs of color and shapes and lines which have no direct bearing to representational concepts but seem to satisfy his need for self-expression as well as a story told with objects and characters.

Children do amazing non-objective painting out of intuitive urges to express joy or energy in painting as free of direct literal terms as are skipping and whistling.

Non-objective art is essentially the expression of rhythmic sensations rather than the expression of ideas or emotions connected with ideas and for that reason it has strong appeal to the child.

Ideas are superimposed upon the young child's already highly developed "feelings" and responses to the visible, tangible world and therefore are not

[153]

native to him. Patterns of things seen and yet unexplained in logical relation to each other are impressed on his mind's eye and easily summoned to his pencil. His scribbles are certainly unconscious statements of those unclassified but clear impressions.

The intelligent, adult, non-objective artist learns to control his purely sensory pattern pictures in such a fashion as to make them orderly, while the child, unable to apply considered elimination or emphasis, scrawls his patterns entirely intuitively.

The source, however, is the same and while the results are vastly improved by the adult, those of most children are lively inventions of fresh minds.

Here is a series of non-objective paintings by six-year-old children They were done at school as part of the regular curriculum.

These children certainly had never had explained to them the aesthetics of art or the subtle theory which leads many painters to abstract and paint non-objectively.

They merely responded to their teacher's suggestion that they paint a "picture" without "things" — just a series of colors and forms that "come into their heads."

The apparent disorder of arrangement, the occasional unbalance, the lack of continuity which are inevitably the result of immaturity do not, however, destroy the validity of the pure emotional quality of these paintings.

Each is a naked mood, as clearly defined as are sulks or frowns, smiles or wonder on the face of a child. To the child psychologist they indicate rich "talent sources" and uninhibited self-expression.

UNINHIBITED SELF-EXPRESSION

DRAMA IN DESIGN RATHER THAN STORY

The dream world interpreted in the symbols of the seen world are the common ingredients of many child drawings. Here are some weird examples of their products. To me they reveal a path to the child mind untraceable by any other means than their pictures. A. Z.

Unintelligible as these may appear at first glance they will, upon examination, carry to you the impact of the high emotionalism involved in their painting.

EMOTIONAL
NON-OBJECTIVES

Asked to do "emotional" non-objective paintings utilizing only dots, dashes or long brush strokes to fill an area with color rhythms, these paintings show the vivid quality of imagination and mood to be brought into play by suggestion, for it is doubtful if these children would have done such things if their value had not been suggested.

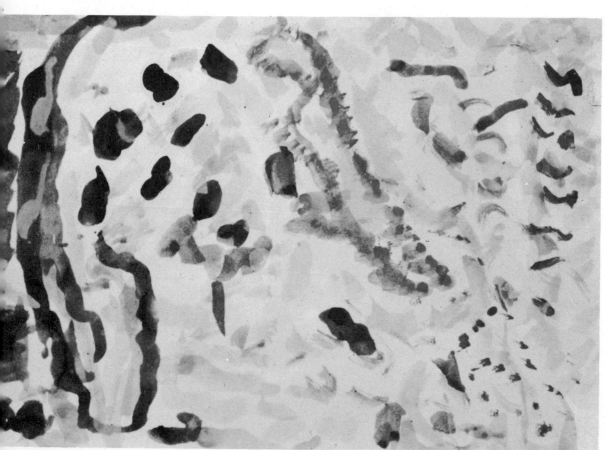

EMOTION IN NON-OBJECTIVE PAINTINGS

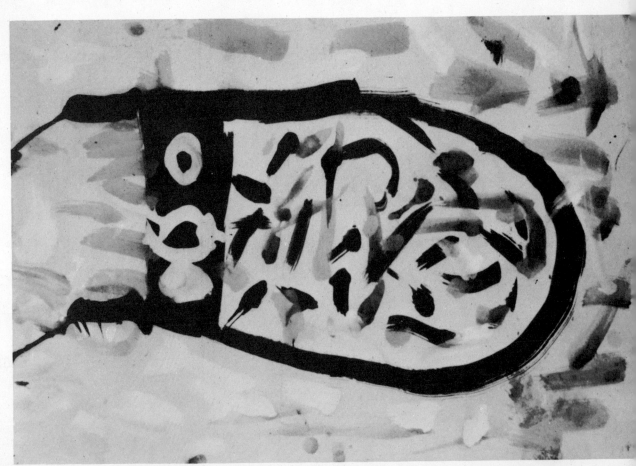

*Some children have a very strong sense of design and in these cases objects have
been used in repetition to make a pattern.*

30. CHILD ABSTRACT PAINTING

ANOTHER ART TERM, abstraction, is not in the vocabulary of a child nor are theories of its adult adherents part of a child's usual education but each child is a natural abstractionist in the purest sense of the word.

To abstract means to take from a figure or objects such parts as will serve to aid the point or emotion to be expressed, eliminate other portions, or stress certain parts and play down others to rearrange and even redesign forms to suit the artist's needs. In doing so, much of the obvious physical realism of the figure or object is lost but the vital character is often enhanced and its relation to the things about it changed from one of main object with background, or principal with props, to a purposeful integration.

Children do not hesitate to enlarge heads or features enormously, elongate limbs, make houses tiny in relation to humans, or animals infinitely larger than they are, in order to express the impression these things make upon them.

They will, perhaps unconsciously, distort and rearrange objects, compelled by emotions the source of which lies deeper than the immediate decision to do these things.

The adult contributes to his abstractions a much greater understanding of purpose but the drive is of the same nature, that of expressing things beyond the limits of the strictly literal.

[165]

ABSTRACTED HOUSES AND TREES

ANIMAL THEMES ABSTRACTED
Always enticing to children as subjects for painting, animals can be used as a theme for designs with background to form a semi-abstract pattern.

This eight-year-old boy integrated a conventionalized airplane into his design with a rare feeling for an all-over pattern. He made the plane's form of no more importance than that of the hills, clouds and sky shapes, all set into a most interesting flat pattern.

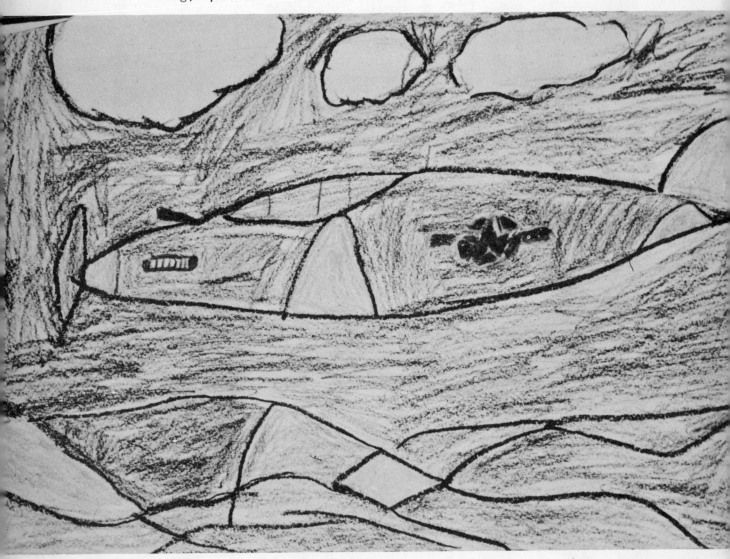

Educational Alliance, New York City

This dramatic and interesting painting is the emotional expression of the impact of death upon a sensitive 6-year-old boy. Interpreted psycho-analytically, the deep band of red above the black mass which represents the grave is a symbol of suffering. But the three living figures, the bright yellow breaking through the bars at the lower right indicate that the child is beginning to recover from his sense of desolation

In this extremely interesting painting, a twelve-year-old girl has employed several fruits and vegetables as a motif for a very free emotional design.

Notice how the well-placed forms of the fruit are brought into closer relation with each other by a spontaneous, moving series of wavy brush strokes.

The large, simplified forms of fruit and the manner of paint application indicate assurance, wit and pleasure involved in the doing.

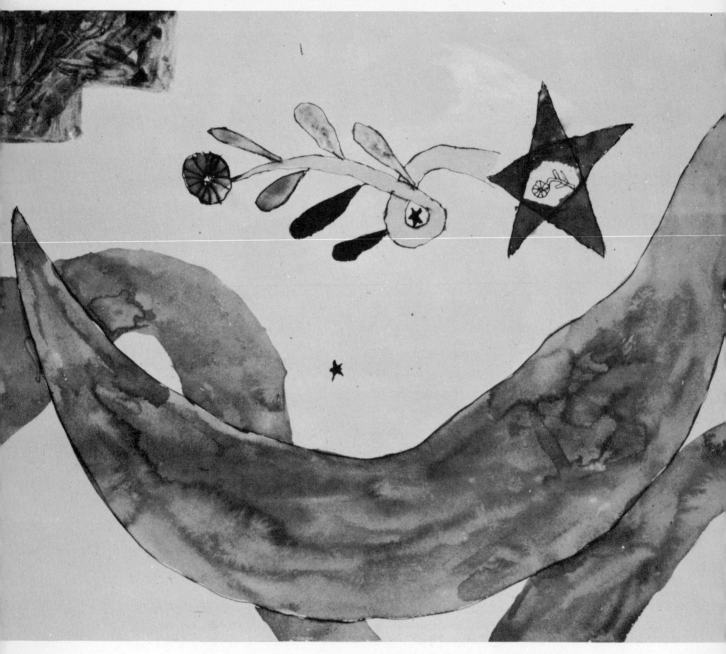

A SURREALIST CONCEPT *full of imagination and movement*

31. CHILD SURREALIST PAINTING

MOST ADULTS are often boastful of being "realists," sure of the sanity and completeness of their vision, never doubting the totality of the objective world available to their five senses.

"Realists" among painters are those who disdain all but the outer appearance of the visual world and the accepted, standardized point of view of that visual world.

The surrealists, or, as they have sometimes been called, the hyperrealists, claim that their approach is truly "real" in that they encompass that which the conscious eye and the inner vision of the subconscious eye behold. For these artists, the world of the external offers only the symbols of communication by means of which they can project their deeper vision.

A child is the supreme realist in that he sees the outer world in its, as yet, uninterpreted form and he portrays it as it appears to him with great subjectivity. His naive viewpoint, coupled with unconscious personal reactions, makes his drawing of what he sees at times very "surrealist" indeed. Lacking the philosophy of surrealism which causes the adult practitioner to be nonconformist and to seek to synthesize the inner world with the outer by decision, children do so by compulsion unknown to them.

[171]

Another dynamic composition. This one is made up of buildings in sharp lines of stress and strain, yet the composition "holds together."

Force and terror unattainable by any means other than this combination of distortion and sharp contrast prompted the always intense Picasso to make this sketch for "Guernica."

[172]

This is a "story picture" of a girl dreaming of school and the things connected with it. Notice the intelligent concept of the dream as related to the sleeping girl. A. Z.

The girl of ten years and her dream is evidently expressing her resentment against school, teacher and regulation, for in the dream enclosed in the circle, she depicts her play life as compared with the picture of the teacher at the board in the upper right hand corner and the child called upon to recite in the lower right hand corner.

School is detested and there is a desire to escape into play life. The school, which is an extension of the home, must also represent the home, the teacher must be equated with mother.

An unhappy, infantile, disturbed child who rebels against growing up, going to school and studying. She would much prefer her dream world. Dr. S. Z. Orgel.

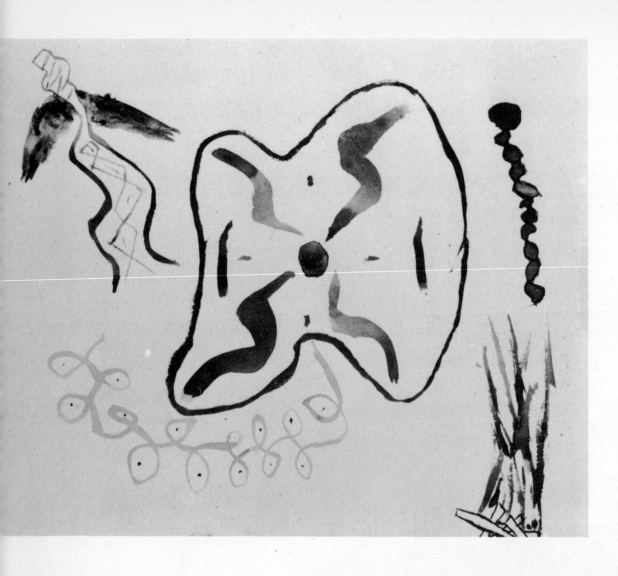

THREE SURREALIST CONCEPTS
CONTAINING REPEATED SYMBOLS

[174]

The high imaginative quality of this witch's tale, painted with great gusto by an eleven-year-old girl, shows an approach to painting to be envied by many a seasoned painter.

Untroubled by any consideration other than the telling of her story with the utmost directness, she has expressed speed, night and the macabre witch with economy, fine flare and fearlessness.

32. CHILD EXPRESSIONISM

THE ADULT Expressionist painter is one by conscious decision. He rejects as valid, for himself at least, any of the other schools and methods as a medium of self-expression. He determines to utilize the pure emotional impulse as a motivating power in his painting.

Children, on the other hand, are natural Expressionists. They make no conscious choice of that school of painting. Emotional expression is the inevitable outlet for their highly egocentric characters. To expect a child to choose any art form other than the pure emotional one would be to endow him with powers of rationalization beyond his years.

It is not to be construed that the adult Expressionist does not utilize the technical and reasoning powers available to followers of other schools of painting and in this respect his emotional expressions are intensified and properly channelized.

The child Expressionist, strong as his emotions are, is inevitably hampered by his lack of resourcefulness in the techniques of telling, but his work is no less authentically of the "Expressionist School" because of that and often such work reaches extremely high standards of pure emotional expression.

[177]

The character of the little seven-year-old girl who created this great study in space and aloneness is clear.

With an economy worthy of a wise adult artist this child has conceived a wasteland, chilly lighted by a pale sun and a weirdly anachronistic moon. Pitifully deposited on the rim of this cold world is an uncertain, frightened little figure waiting, apparently, for the nameless terrors lurking beyond the frame of the picture, waiting hopelessly and helplessly.

Discoverable in this powerful expressionist work is a potentially fine artist, full of passion and capable of expressing it in terms to be envied by any but the greatest artists. A. Z.

This crayon drawing by a seven-year-old girl evidently expresses her extreme fearfulness. She is frightened, shy and withdrawn. She feels all alone in the great vastness of her world which she feels unable to cope with adequately. Her attitude in the drawing bespeaks depression and a fear of dying for lack of the love she needs and must have to survive. The skull head symbolizes death. The vastness—loneliness. Her standing on a thin line, the precariousness of her position and the imminence of death without the needed love and protection. This child seems very ill and greatly in need of love and attention. I would suspect that this child is either an adopted or unwanted child who feels the rejecting forces of her unhappy environment. Dr. S. Z. Orgel.

This group of talented youngsters in the sketch class at the Silvermine (Conn.) Guild of Artists shows how the guidance of competent instructors can channel towards skilled maturity the talents which you have helped develop by working with your child at home. With Gail Symon and Shirley Kaplan encouraging their experimental efforts, these children are already working in oil, charcoal, tempera and pastels.

33. SEEING ART AND COLLECTING PICTURES

ONE OF THE MOST STIMULATING EXPERIENCES for a parent is to listen to the reactions of his child to fine paintings. Unencumbered by the snobberies with which the adult approaches "name" paintings, snobberies which have perverted his judgment out of all objectivity, the child looks at a picture and judges it entirely on the basis of its effect upon him.

Of course I speak here of the child above the age of six, when he has reached the stage of articulate speech. His "opinion" of the picture seen will have no validity as artistic criticism, his judgment, of course, will not be mature, considered or "right," but — and this is the factor most difficult to find in adults — it will be honest. The impact of the picture, in its most elemental character, will be registered on the child and his response will be especially interesting.

As to the type of pictures to which the child should be exposed I wish to be emphatic. Censorship, whether on moral or aesthetic grounds is always wrong on two major counts. The first is the arbitrary limiting of experiences in childhood which never again can have quite the profound emotional meaning in the multi-experience, divided-interest days of adult life.

Second is the inevitable influence by omission which a "picked" art range, based on your prejudices, will produce. When you examine your own struggles to outgrow the effects of bad taste of your own mentors at one time or another, you will be less inclined to force your child's tastes by restricting experience. This does not mean that the tawdry should be given the same place in the artistic life of your child, as the fine. He will be exposed to the vulgar and cheap in art through the press, magazines and comic books without your help.

He should see and, if possible, be surrounded in his home, by the pictures of all the "schools" of art from the classic to the extreme modern. The conglomerate will synthesize to form his own aesthetic tastes as he grows older. If it is not asking too much of you, try to familiarize yourself with these various schools of art and try to understand the intentions and philosophies which underlie them both for his good and your own, for he will ask questions and you should be prepared to answer.

When you tell him that a picture is, in your opinion, good or bad, you should also be able to tell him why and ask his opinion. Your criticisms will only have validity for him and yourself if you have understood the aims of the artist.

The chief source of his education in fine paintings is of course, the museums. These, however, are only in the big cities and even there the curious hours they are kept open — when most men are at work and children are at school — make them only an occasional art experience.

It is important to have available and conspicuous some good art at all times. A fine collection of prints, in color and black and white, can easily be collected from the magazine and newspaper art sections. Why not make a file of each period of art, classified according to country and "school." Enlist your child's aid in making the collection. Tack up the ones you and he like best and discuss them. A wide, liberal education lies in the panorama of painting through the years—not only aesthetic, but historic, political, moral and social. Both of you will profit immeasurably in the process of building this collection, infinitely more rewarding than collecting bottle tops or match cases or even coins and stamps.

Painted in classes of the W.P.A. Federal Art Project, now on loan to the Museum of Modern Art, New York.

Robinson Crusoe as a Young Man, remarkably reminiscent of Winslow Homer's *The Gulf Stream,* is the work of a thirteen-year-old Washington, D. C. boy.

34. GALLERY OF CHILDREN'S DRAWINGS AND PAINTINGS

IT MUST BE STRESSED that the work by children reprinted here is not unique. Work is being done in elementary schools all over the world that is equal and in special cases better. The quantity of excellent drawing and painting is enormous and, except for the rare "child art" shown in museums, completely ignored by the adult "art lovers."

Their grounds for ignoring these most interesting manifestations are in some respects understandable. Most people, this writer included, are repelled by the public performances of precocious children. The unhappy child who is persuaded to sing adult songs or play the piano as a virtuoso is only slightly less unhappy than is his adult audience, with the possible exception of a doting mother.

A cute recitation by a clever moppet has the faculty of depressing me for hours. Children in the movies and on the radio when called upon to "act" bring on acute nausea.

Though I do not hold with the old school of adult adage makers that "children should be seen and not heard," there is much to be said for the maxim when used in relation to the performing child.

However, insofar as the child is being a child and giving forth with the abilities natural to his years, experience and inner development, his art "performances" are legitimate. He is not cutely aping an adult activity but speaking freely his own language and he has things to say.

Those adults who, through prejudice, cut themselves off from this pleasure are missing a rich experience and a source of improved understanding of their own child.

[183]

Some remarkable examples of child art from various European museums are shown on this and the following pages. It should be noted that American children — perhaps, indeed your own child — have painted many works of equal merit.

[185]

Paysage d'hiver

[187]

THE FOLLOWING LIST OF REPRESENTATIVE ART CENTERS, SCHOOLS AND
COLLEGES HAS BEEN COMPILED WITH A VIEW TOWARD HELPING THE
PARENTS OF CHILDREN WHO HAVE SHOWN A DESIRE TO GO ON
WITH THEIR ART STUDIES

ALABAMA
Montgomery Museum of Art, 205 High St.;
two-week school

ARIZONA
Phoenix Fine Art Association, Heard Museum;
Saturday classes

ARKANSAS
Hendrix College, Conway, Ark.; once wk., free
children's classes

CALIFORNIA
La Jolla Art Center, 610 Prospect St.; classes in
painting, ceramics, weaving
Oakland-Art League of East Bay, Oakland Art
Gallery, Municipal Auditorium, 12th and
Fallon Sts.
Palo Alto Art Club, 340 Melville St.
Richmond Art Center, 237 9th St.
Fine Arts Society of San Diego, Balboa Park
San Francisco Art Assoc., 800 Chestnut St.;
Saturday classes
Santa Barbara Museum of Art, State and Ana-
pamu Sts.

COLORADO
Gilpin County Arts Assoc., Central City, P.O.
Box 691; classes in July and Aug.
Colo. Springs Fine Arts Center, 30 W. Dale St.
Chapell House, 1330 Logan St., Denver

CONNECTICUT
Wadsworth Atheneum, 25 Atheneum Square,
Hartford
Mystic Art Association, Mystic; Sat. morning
classes
Lyman Allyn Museum, 100 Mohegan Ave., New
London
Silvermine Guild of Artists, Silvermine; pottery
classes
Stamford Museum, Courtland Park
Institute of Commercial Art, Westport; Cor-
respondence Art Courses

DELAWARE
Rehoboth Art League, Henlopen Acres, Reho-
both Beach; summer classes
Wilmington, Delaware Art Center, Park Dr. at
Woodlawn Ave.

FLORIDA
Bradenton Art Gallery, 529 13th St.
Clearwater Museum School of Art, Chamber of
Commerce Bldg.

GEORGIA
Gertrude Herbert Institute of Art, 506 Talfair
St., Augusta

ILLINOIS
Art Institute of Chicago, Michigan at Adams St.;
sketch classes to children of members
South Side Community Art Center, 3831 Michi-
gan Ave.; free recreational art classes
Elgin Academy Art Gallery, Laura Davidson
Sears Academy of Fine Arts; child. class
Joliet Artists League, 73 W. Van Buren St.
Austin, Oak Park and River Forest League, 720
Chicago Ave., Oak Park
Rockford Art Association, Burpee Art Gallery,
737 N. Main St.; children's classes and Junior
group for high school boys and girls
Springfield Art Association, Edwards Place
North Shore Art League, Community House,
Winnetka

INDIANA
Evansville Public Museum, 216 N.W. 2nd St.
Art School of John Herron Art Institute, 16th
and Pennsylvania Sts., Indianapolis; children's and high school classes

IOWA
Davenport, Municipal Art Gallery, 120 W. 5th
St.

KANSAS
Wichita Art Association, 401 N. Belmont Ave.

LOUISIANA
Terrebonne Art League, 119 2nd St., Houma
Art Association of New Orleans, Delgado Mu-
seum, City Park; Sat. classes for ages 9-17

MAINE
Brick Store Museum, 117 Main St., Kennebunk
Portland Society of Art, Sweat Memorial Art
Museum, 111 High St.

MARYLAND
Maryland Institute of Fine and Practical Arts,
Mt. Royal Ave., Baltimore 17; summer school,
6 weeks

MASSACHUSETTS
Beverly Historical Society, 117 Cabot St.,
Beverly
Children's Art Centre, 36 Rutland St., Boston
Institute of Contemporary Art, 130 Newbury
St., Boston

Museum of Fine Arts, Huntington Ave., Boston; Saturday classes

Fitchburg Art Centre, Merriam Parkway, Fitchburg

George Walter Vincent Smith Art Museum, 222 State St., Springfield

Worcester Art Museum, 55 Salisbury St., Worcester

MICHIGAN

Grand Rapids Art Gallery, 230 E. Fulton St., Grand Rapids

Hackley Art Gallery, Muskegon

Saginaw Museum, 1126 N. Michigan Ave., Saginaw

Walker Art Center School, 1710 Lyndale Ave., S., Minneapolis; 17 wk. course for children

MINNESOTA

Rochester Art Centre, Rochester

St. Paul Gallery and Art School, 476 Summit Ave.

MISSOURI

Kansas City Art Institute, 4415 Warwick Blvd.

NEBRASKA

Joslyn Memorial Art Museum, 2218 Dodge St., Omaha

NEW HAMPSHIRE

Manchester Institute of Arts and Sciences, 148 Concord St.

NEW JERSEY

Englewood Art Gallery, 28 N. Van Brunt St.

Newark Art Club, 38 Franklin St.

Rahway Art Center, 265 Hamilton St.

NEW MEXICO

Roosevelt County Fine Arts Society, Portales, New Mexico

NEW YORK

Cayuga Museum of History and Art, 203 Genesee St., Auburn, N. Y.

Albright Art School, 1231 Elmwood Ave., Buffalo

Cooperstown Children's Museum, Library Building; children from 6-15

Arnot Art Gallery, 235 Lake St., Elmira, N. Y.; 2 week classes for children

Brooklyn Museum, Eastern Parkway and Washington Ave.

Metropolitan Museum, 5th Ave., and 82nd.; Junior Museum, N. Y. C.

Museum of Modern Art, 11 W. 53rd St., N. Y. C.

Educational Alliance, E. Broadway and Jefferson St.; free afternoon classes in fine arts and arts and crafts

Syracuse Museum of Fine Arts, 407 James St., Syracuse; after school and Sat. morns.

NORTH CAROLINA

Charlotte—Mint Museum of Art, 510 Hempstead Place, Eastover

OHIO

Cincinnati Art Museum, Eden Park

Cleveland Art Museum, East. Blvd. and Bellflower Rd.

Columbus Gallery of Fine Arts, 480 E. Broad St.

Dayton Art Institute, Forest and Riverview Aves.

Toledo Museum, Monroe St.

Butler Art Institute, 524 Wick Ave., Youngstown, Ohio

Art Institute of Zanesville, Maple Ave.

OKLAHOMA

Philbrook Art Centre, 2727 S. Rockford Rd., Tulsa

OREGON

Lincoln County Art Center, Delake

Portland Museum Art School, West Park and Madison

PENNSYLVANIA

Art Association of Harrisburg; Sat. classes, and evening classes for older children

Philadelphia Museum of Art, Parkway at 26th

University Museum, Univ. of Penn., 33rd and Spruce

Abstract Group of Pittsburgh, Arts and Crafts Center, 5th and Shady Aves.

Carnegie Institute, 4400 Forbes St.

Everhart Museum of Natural History, Science and Art, Scranton

Martin Memorial Library and Gallery, 159 Market St., York

TEXAS

Abilene Museum of Fine Arts

Dallas Museum of Fine Arts

Fort Worth Art Association, Public Library

Museum of Fine Arts of Houston, Main and Montrose Blvd.

VERMONT

University of Vermont, Burlington

VIRGINIA

Virginia Museum of Fine Arts, Grove Ave., and Boulevard, Richmond

WASHINGTON

Music and Art Foundation, 311 Medical Arts Bldg., Seattle

WISCONSIN

Milwaukee Art Institute, 772 N. Jefferson St., Milwaukee

Charles A. Wustum Museum of Fine Arts, 2542 Northwestern Ave., Racine